# Prophet of Darkness

*Other books by Richard Wurmbrand*

Answer to Moscow's Bible
Christ on the Jewish Road
If that were Christ, would you give him your blanket?
If Prison Walls Could Speak
In God's Underground
Little Notes That Like Each Other
One Hundred Prison Meditations
Reaching Towards the Heights
Sermons in Solitary Confinement
Stronger than Prison Walls
The Underground Saints
The Wurmbrand Letters
Tortured for Christ
Was Marx a Satanist?
Where Christ is Tortured
Where Christ Still Suffers

# Marx:
# Prophet of Darkness

Communism's hidden forces revealed

# RICHARD WURMBRAND

Marshall Pickering

Marshall Morgan and Scott
Marshall Pickering
3 Beggarwood Lane,
Basingstoke, Hants RG23 7LP, UK

First published in 1986 by Marshall Morgan
and Scott Publications Ltd
Part of the Marshall Pickering Holdings Group
A subsidiary of the Zondervan Corporation

*British Library Cataloguing in Publication Data*

Wurmbrand, Richard
  Marx: prophet of darkness.
  1. Communism and religion  2. Communism
  3. Satanism
  I. Title
  335.4    HX536

ISBN 0–551–01313–3

Phototypeset in Linotron Palatino by
Input Typesetting Ltd, London
Printed in Great Britain by
Hazell Watson and Viney Ltd,
Member of the BPCC Group,
Aylesbury, Bucks

# Introduction to the 5th Enlarged Edition

This work started as a small brochure containing only hints about possible connections between Marxism and the Satanist church.

No one had ventured to write about this before. Therefore I was cautious, even timid.

But in the course of time more and more evidence accumulated in my files. Let the reader judge!

Marxism today governs over one third of mankind. If it could be shown that the originators and perpetrators of this movement in history were secretly devil-worshippers, consciously exploiting Satanic powers, the mere thought would chill the marrow and cause even worldlings to blanch. The occult—even in so-called art forms—is meant to terrorise.

If some were to reject my thesis—the theme of this book—out of hand, it would not surprise me. Science and technology, advance at a rapid pace because we are always ready to scrap obsolescent machinery in favour of new conveniences. Not so in the field of sociology or religion. Ideas die hard, and a mind set, unlike a computer chip, is not easily altered or replaced. Even fresh evidence may fail to persuade. The doors of some minds have rusty hinges.

But I do bring added proofs to support my thesis. I invite you to consider them.

The Communists have certainly taken note of this book, which has been translated into Russian, Chinese, Romanian, German, Czech, and other languages, and has been smuggled into these Iron Curtain countries in great quantities.

For instance, the East Berlin journal *Deutsche Lehrer-*

*zeitung*, under the heading 'The Killer of Marx', denounced it vehemently, calling it 'the most broadly based, provocative, and heinous work written against Marx.'

Can Marx be so easily destroyed? Is this his Achilles' heel? Would Marxism be discredited if men knew about his connection with Satanism? Do enough people care?

Marxism is *the* great fact of modern life. Whatever your opinion of it, whether or not you believe in the existence of Satan, whatever importance you attach to the cult of Satan practised in certain circles, I ask you to consider, weigh, and judge the documentation I present.

I believe it will help you orient yourself to the problems with which Marxism confronts every inhabitant of the globe today.


RICHARD WURMBRAND

# 1: Devil's Advocate

## Marx's Christian Writings

Before becoming an economist and a Communist of renown, Marx was a humanist. Today one third of the world is Marxist. Marxism in one form or another is embraced by many in Capitalist countries, too. There are Christians, even clergymen, some of high standing, who are sure that while Jesus might have had the right answers about how to get to heaven, Marx had the right answers about how to help the hungry, destitute, and oppressed on earth.

Marx, it is said, was deeply humane. He was dominated by one idea: how to help the exploited masses. What impoverishes them, he maintained, is capitalism. Once this rotten system is overthrown, after a transitional period of dictatorship of the proletariat, a society will emerge in which everyone will work according to his abilities in factories and farms belonging to the collective, and will be rewarded according to his needs. There will be no state to rule over the individual, no wars, no revolutions, only an everlasting, universal brotherhood.

In order for the masses to achieve happiness, more is needed beyond the mere overthrow of Capitalism. Marx writes: 'The abolition of religion as the illusory happiness of man is a requisite for their real happiness. The call to abandon their illusions about their conditions is a call to abandon a condition which requires illusions. The criticism of religion is, therefore, the criticism of this vale of tears of which religion is the halo.'[1]

Marx was anti-religious because religion obstructs the fulfilment of the Communist ideal which he considered the only answer to the world's problems. This is how Marxists explain their position.

There are clergymen who explain it in the same way. The English clergyman Rev. Oestreicher said in a sermon: 'Communism, whatever its present varied forms of expression, both good and bad, is in origin a movement for the emancipation of man from exploitation by his fellow man. Sociologically, the Church was and largely still is on the side of the world's exploiters. Karl Marx, whose theories only thinly veil a passion for justice and brotherhood that has its roots in the Hebrew prophets, loathed religion because it was used as an instrument to perpetuate a status quo in which children were slaves and worked to death in order to make others rich here in Britain. It was no cheap jibe a hundred years ago to say that religion was the opium of the masses . . . As members of the Body of Christ we must come in simple penitence knowing that we owe a deep debt to every Communist.'[2]

Marxism makes an impression on people's thinking because of its success, but success proves nothing. Witch doctors often succeed, too. Success confirms error as well as truth. Failure is often priceless, because it can open the way to deeper truth. So an analysis of some of Marx's works should be made without regard to their success.

In his early youth, Karl Marx was a Christian. His first written work is called *The Union of the Faithful with Christ*. There we read these beautiful words 'Through love of Christ we turn our hearts at the same time toward our brethren who are inwardly bound to us and for whom He gave Himself in sacrifice.'

So Marx knew a way for men to become loving brethren toward one another. It is Christianity.

He continues: 'Union with Christ could give an inner elevation, comfort in sorrow, calm trust, and a heart susceptible to human love, to everything noble and great, not for the sake of ambition and glory, but only for the sake of Christ.'[3]

At approximately the same time Marx writes in his thesis, *Considerations of a Young Man in Choosing His Career:* 'Religion itself teaches us that the Ideal toward which all strive sacrificed Himself for humanity, and who shall dare contradict such claims? If we have chosen the position in which we can accomplish the most for Him, then we can never be crushed by burdens, because they are only sacrifices made for the sake of all.'[4]

However, it is necessary to observe that in his thesis upon finishing high school he repeated six times the word 'destroy', which not even one of his colleagues used in this exam. 'Destroy' then became his nickname. It was natural for him to want to destroy because he spoke about mankind as 'human trash' and said, 'No man visits me and I like this, because present mankind may [an obscenity]. They are a bunch of rascals.'

No conversion or apostasy changes a man one hundred percent. Sometimes after such a reversal of thinking, the old beliefs or disbeliefs thrust themselves into one's awareness, revealing that they are not erased from the pages of the mind but only repressed into the subconscious. The old Christ-complex appears in Marx's writings long after he changed into a militant fighter against religion.

Even in an abstruse book of political economy like *The Capital*, in which reflections about religion are obviously of little concern, the mature and anti-religious Marx writes, entirely out of context, 'Christianity with its cultus of abstract man, more especially in its bourgeois developments, Protestantism, Deism, etc., is the most fitting form of religion.'[5]

Remember, Marx started out as a Christian believer. When he finished high school, the following was written on his graduation certificate under the heading 'Religious Knowledge': 'His knowledge of the Christian faith and morals is fairly clear and well grounded. He knows also to some extent the history of the Christian church.'[6]

## Marx's First Anti-God Writings

Shortly after Marx received this certificate, something mysterious happened in his life: he became profoundly passionately anti-religious. A new Marx began to emerge.

He writes in a poem, 'I wish to avenge myself against the One who rules above.'[7] So he was convinced that there is 'One above who rules.' He was in a quarrel with him. But the One above had done him no wrong. Marx belonged to a relatively well-to-do family. He had not hungered in his childhood. He was much better off than many fellow students. What produced this terrible hatred for God?

No personal motive is known. Was Karl Marx in this declaration only someone else's mouthpiece? At an age when every normal young man has beautiful dreams of doing good to others and preparing a career for himself, why should he have written the following lines in his poem *Invocation of One in Despair*?

> So a god has snatched from me my all
> In the curse and rack of destiny.
> All his worlds are gone beyond recall!
> Nothing but revenge is left to me!
>
> I shall build my throne high overhead,
> Cold, tremendous shall its summit be.
> For its bulwark—superstitious dread.
> For its marshal—blackest agony.
>
> Who looks on it with a healthy eye

*Shall turn back, deathly pale and dumb.*
*Clutched by blind and chill mortality.*
*May his happiness prepare its tomb.*[8]

Marx dreamt about ruining the world created by God. In another poem he wrote:

*Then I will be able to walk triumphantly,*
*Like a god, through the ruins of their kingdom.*
*Every word of mine is fire and action.*
*My breast is equal to that of the Creator.*[9]

The words 'I shall build my throne high overhead' and the confession that from the one sitting on this throne will emanate only dread and agony remind us of Lucifer's proud boast: 'I will ascend into heaven, I will exalt my throne above the stars of God' (Isaiah 14:13).

Perhaps it is no coincidence that Bakunin, who was for a time one of his most intimate friends, wrote: 'One has to worship Marx in order to be loved by him. One has at least to fear him in order to be tolerated by him . . . Marx is extremely proud, up to dirt and madness.'[9a]

## The Satanist Church and Oulanem

But why does Marx wish such a throne?

The answer is found in a little-known drama which he also composed during his student years. It is called *Oulanem*. To explain this title a digression is needed.

One of the rituals of the Satanist Church is the black mass, which Satanist priests recite at midnight. Black candles are put in the candlestick upside down. The priest is dressed in his ornate robes, but with the lining outside.

11

He says all things prescribed in the prayer book, but reads from the end towards the beginning. The holy names of God, Jesus, and Mary are read inversely. A crucifix is fastened upside down or trampled upon. The body of a naked woman serves as an altar. A consecrated wafer stolen from some church is inscribed with the name 'Satan' and is used for a mock-Communion. During the black mass a Bible is burned. All those present promise to commit the seven deadly sins, as enumerated in Catholic catechisms, and never to do any good. An orgy follows.

Devil worship is very old. The Bible has much to say about—and against—it.

For example, the Jews, though entrusted by God with the true religion, sometimes faltered in their faith and then 'sacrificed unto devils' (Deuteronomy 32:17). At one time, King Jeroboam of Israel ordained priests for the devils (II Chronicles 11:15).

So from time immemorial men have believed in the existence of the devil. Sin and wickedness are the hallmark of his kingdom, disintegration and destruction its logical result. The great concentrations of evil design in times past as well as in modern Communism and Nazism would have been impossible without a guiding force, the devil himself. He has been the mastermind, the secret agent, supplying the unifying energy in his grand scheme to control mankind.

Characteristically, *Oulanem* is an inversion of a holy name: it is an anagram of Emmanuel, Biblical name for Jesus, which means in Hebrew 'God is with us.' Such inversions of names are considered effective in black magic.

We will be able to understand the drama *Oulanem* only in the light of a strange confession that Marx made in a poem called *The Player*, later downplayed by both himself and his followers:

*The hellish vapours rise and fill the brain,*
*Till I go mad and my heart is utterly changed.*
*See this sword?*
*The prince of darkness*
*Sold it to me.*
*For me he beats the time and gives the signs.*
*Ever more boldly I play the dance of death.*[10]

These lines take on special significance when we learn that in the rites of higher initiation in the Satanist cult an 'enchanted' sword which ensures success is sold to the candidate. He pays for it by signing a covenant, with blood taken from his wrists, that his soul will belong to Satan after death.

To enable the reader to grasp the horrid intent of these poems, I should mention—though with natural revulsion—that *The Satanic Bible*, after saying 'the crucifix symbolises pallid incompetence hanging on a tree', calls Satan 'the ineffable Prince of Darkness who rules the earth.' As opposed to 'the lasting foulness of Bethlehem', 'the cursed Nazarene', 'the impotent king', 'fugitive and mute god', 'vile and abhorred pretender to the majesty of Satan', the devil is called 'the God of Light', with angels 'cowering and trembling with fear and prostrating themselves before him' and 'sending Christian minions staggering to their doom.'

Now I quote from the drama *Oulanem:*

*And they are also Oulanem, Oulanem.*
*The name rings forth like death, rings forth*
*Until it dies away in a wretched crawl.*
*Stop, I've got it now! It rises from my soul*
*As clear as air, as strong as my own bones.*[11]

*Yet I have power within my youthful arms*
*To clench and crush you [i.e. personified*
  *humanity] with tempestuous force,*
*While for us both the abyss yawns in darkness.*

*You will sink down and I shall follow laughing,*
*Whispering in your ears, 'Descend,*
   *come with me, friend.'*[12]

The Bible, which Marx had studied in his high school years and which he knew quite well in his mature years, says that the devil will be bound by an angel and cast into the bottomless pit (*abyssos* in Greek: see Revelation 20:3). Marx desires to draw the whole of mankind into this pit reserved for the devil and his angels.

Who speaks through Marx in this drama? Is it reasonable to expect a young student to entertain as his life's dream the vision of mankind entering into the abyss of darkness ('outer darkness' is a Biblical expression for 'hell') and himself laughing as he follows those he has led to unbelief? Nowhere in the world is this ideal cultivated except in the initiation rites of the Satanist church, at its highest degrees.

The time comes for Oulanem's death. His words are:

*Ruined, ruined. My time has clean run out.*
*The clock has stopped, the pygmy house has crumbled.*
*Soon I shall embrace eternity to my breast, and soon*
*I shall howl gigantic curses on mankind.*[13]

Marx had loved the words of Mephistopheles in *Faust*, 'Everything in existence is worth being destroyed.' Everything—including the proletariat and the comrades. Marx quoted these words in *The 18th Brumaire*.[14] Stalin acted on them and destroyed even his own family.

In *Faust*, Satan is called the spirit that denies everything. This is precisely Marx's attitude. He writes about 'pitiless criticism of all that exists', 'war against the situation in Germany', 'merciless criticism of all', 'It is the first duty of the press to undermine the foundations of the existing political system.'[14a]

Marx said about himself that he is 'the most outstanding hater of the so-called positive.'[14b]

The Satanist sect is not materialistic. It believes in eternal life. Oulanem, the person through whom Marx speaks, does not contest it. He asserts eternal life but as a life of hate magnified to its extreme. It is worth noting that eternity for the devils means 'torment.' Thus Jesus was reproached by the demons: 'Are you come hither to torment us before our time?' (Matthew 8:29).

Marx is similarly obsessed:

> *Ha! Eternity! She is our eternal grief,*
> *An indescribable and immeasurable Death,*
> *Vile artificiality conceived to scorn us,*
> *Ourselves being clockwork, blindly mechanical,*
> *Made to be the fool-calendars of Time and Space,*
> *Having no purpose save to happen, to be ruined,*
> *So that there shall be something to ruin.*[15]

We begin to understand what has happened to young Marx. He had had Christian convictions but had not led a consistent life. His correspondence with his father testifies to his squandering great sums of money on pleasures and his constant quarrelling with parental authority about this and other matters. Then he seems to have fallen in with the tenets of the highly secret Satanist church and received the rites of initiation. Satan, whom his worshippers see in their hallucinatory orgies, speaks through them. Thus Marx is only Satan's mouthpiece when he utters in his poem *Invocation of One in Despair* the words, 'I wish to avenge myself against the One who rules above.'

Listen to the end of *Oulanem*:

> *If there is a Something which devours,*
> *I'll leap within it, though I bring the*
> *    world to ruins—*

15

*The world which bulks between me*
   *and the abyss*
*I will smash to pieces with my*
   *enduring curses.*

*I'll throw my arms around its harsh reality:*
*Embracing me, the world will dumbly*
   *pass away,*
*And then sink down to utter nothingness,*
*Perished, with no existence—that would be*
   *really living.*[16]

Marx was probably inspired by the words of the Marquis de Sade: 'I abhor nature. I would like to split its planet, hinder its process, stop the circles of stars, overthrow the globes that float in space, destroy what serves nature, protect what harms it—in a word, I wish to insult it in my works . . . Perhaps we will be able to attack the sun, deprive the universe of it, or use it to set the world on fire. These would be real crimes.'

De Sade and Marx propagate the same ideas.

Honest men, as well as men inspired by God, often seek to serve their fellow men by writing books to increase their store of knowledge, improve their morality, stimulate religious sentiments, or at least provide relaxation and amusement.

The devil is the only being who consciously purveys only evil to humankind, through his elect servants.

As far as I know, Marx is the only renowned author who has ever called his own writings 'shit,' 'swinish books.'[16a] He consciously gives his readers filth. No wonder, then, that his disciples, the Communists in Romania and Mozambique, forced prisoners to eat their own excrement and drink their own urine.[16b]

In *Oulanem* Marx does what the devil does: he consigns the entire human race to damnation.

*Oulanem* is probably the only drama in the world

in which all the characters are aware of their own corruption, which they flaunt and celebrate with conviction. In this drama there is no black and white. There exist no Claudius and Ophelia, Iago and Desdemona. Here all are black and all reveal aspects of Mephistopheles. All are satanic, corrupt, and doomed.

## Satan in Marx's Family

When he wrote these things, Marx, a premature genius, was eighteen. His life's programme had thus already been established. There was no word about serving mankind, the proletariat, or socialism. He wished to bring the world to ruin. He wished to build for himself a throne whose bulwark would be human shudder.

At that stage, we find some cryptic passages in the correspondence between Karl Marx and his father. The son writes, 'A curtain had fallen. My holy of holies was rent asunder and new gods had to be installed.'[17] These words were written on 10 November 1837, by a young man who had professed Christianity until then. He had declared that Christ was in his heart. Now this is no longer so. Who are the new gods installed in his place?

The father replies, 'I refrained from insisting on an explanation about a very mysterious matter although it seemed highly dubious.'[18] What was this mysterious matter? Till now no biographer of Marx has explained these strange sentences.

On 2 March 1837, Marx's father writes to his son: 'Your advancement, the dear hope of seeing your name someday of great repute, and your earthly well-being are not the only desires of my heart. These are illusions I had had a long time, but I can assure you that their fulfilment would not have made me happy. Only if your heart remains pure and beats humanly and if *no demon* is able to alienate your heart from better feelings, only then will I be happy.'[19]

What made a father suddenly express the fear of demonic influence upon a young son who until then had been a confessed Christian? Was it the poems he received as a present from his son for his 55th birthday?

The following quotation is taken from Marx's poem *On Hegel*:

> *Words I teach all mixed up into a*
> *devilish muddle.*
> *Thus, anyone may think just what he*
> *chooses to think.*[20]

Here also are words from another epigram on *Hegel*:

> *Because I discovered the highest,*
> *And because I found the deepest through*
> *meditation,*
> *I am great like a God;*
> *I clothe myself in darkness like Him.*[21]

In his poem *The Pale Maiden*, he writes:

> *Thus heaven I've forfeited,*
> *I know it full well.*
> *My soul, once true to God,*
> *Is chosen for hell.*[22]

No commentary is needed.

Marx had started out with artistic ambitions. His poems and drama are important in revealing the state of his heart, but having no literary value they received no recognition. Lack of success in drama gave us a Goebbels, the propaganda minister of the Nazis; in philosophy a Rosenberg, the purveyor of German racism; in painting and architecture a Hitler.

Hitler was a poet too. It can be assumed that he

never read Marx's poetry, but the resemblance is striking. In his poems, he mentions the same Satanist practices. I quote one:

> *On rough nights, I go sometimes*
> *To the oak of Wotan in the still garden,*
> *To make a pact with dark forces.*
> *The moonlight makes runes appear.*
> *Those that were sunbathed during the day*
> *Become small before the magic formula . . .* [23]

Wotan is the chief god of German heathen mythology. Runes were the signs used for writing in olden times.

Hitler soon abandoned a poetic career. So did Marx, who exchanged it for the career of revolutionary in the name of Satan against a society which had not appreciated his poems. This is conceivably one of the motives for his total rebellion. Being despised as a Jew was another.

Two years after his father's expressed concern, in 1839, the young Marx wrote *The Difference Between Democritus' and Epicurus' Philosophy of Nature*, in the preface to which he aligns himself with the declaration of Aeschylus, 'I harbour hatred against all gods.'[24] This he qualifies by stating that he is against all gods on earth and in heaven that do not recognise human selfconsciousness as the supreme godhead.

Marx was an avowed enemy of all gods, a man who had bought his sword from the prince of darkness at the price of his soul. He had declared it his aim to draw all mankind into the abyss and to follow laughing.

Might Marx really have bought his sword from Satan?

His daughter Eleanor says that Marx told her and her sisters many stories when they were children. The one she liked most was about a certain Hans Röckle. 'The telling of the story lasted months and months, because it was a long, long story and never finished. Hans Röckle was a witch . . . who had a shop with toys and many debts . . . though he was a witch, he was always in financial need. Therefore he had to sell against his will all his beautiful things, piece after piece, to the devil . . . some of these adventures were horrifying and made your hair stand on end.'[25]

Is it normal for a father to tell his little children horrifying stories about selling one's dearest treasures to the devil? Robert Payne in his book *Marx*[26] also recounts this incident in great detail, as told by Eleanor: how unhappy Röckle, the magician, sold the toys with reluctance, holding on to them till the last moment. But since he had made a pact with the devil, there was no escaping it.

Marx's biographer continues, 'There can be very little doubt that those interminable stories were autobiographical . . . He had the devil's view of the world, and the devil's malignity. Sometimes he seemed to know that he was accomplishing works of evil.'[27]

When Marx had finished *Oulanem* and his other early poems in which he writes about having a pact with the devil, he had no thought of Socialism. He even fought against it. He was editor of a German magazine, the *Rheinische Zeitung*, which 'does not concede even theoretical validity to Communist ideas in their present form, let alone desire their practical realisation, which it anyway finds impossible . . . Attempts by masses to carry out Communist ideas can be answered by a cannon as soon as they have become dangerous . . .'[28]


## Marx Will Chase God from Heaven

After reaching this stage in his thinking, Marx met Moses Hess, the man who played the most important role in his life, the one who made him embrace the Socialist ideal.

Hess calls him 'Dr Marx my idol, who will give the last kick to medieval religion and politics.'[29] So, to give a kick to religion was his first aim, not Socialism.

Georg Jung, another friend of Marx at that time, writes in 1841 even more clearly that Marx will surely chase God from his heaven and will even sue him. Marx calls Christianity one of the most immoral religions.[30] No wonder, for Marx believed that Christians of ancient times had slaughtered men and eaten their flesh.

These then were the expectations of those who initiated Marx into the depths of Satanism. It was not at all true that Marx entertained lofty social ideals about helping mankind, that religion was a hindrance in fulfilling this ideal, and that for this reason Marx embraced an anti-religious attitude. On the contrary, Marx hated all gods; he hated any notion of God. He was willing to be the man who would kick out God—all this before he had embraced Socialism, which was only the bait to entice proletarians and intellectuals to embrace this devilish ideal.

Eventually Marx claimed not to admit the existence of a Creator. However stupid this may seem, he maintained that mankind shaped itself. He wrote, 'Seeing that for the Socialist man all of so-called world history is nothing other than the creation of man through human work, than the development of nature for man, he has the incontestable proof of his being born from himself . . . The criticism of religion ends with the teaching that man is the supreme being for man.'

When no Creator is acknowledged, there is no one to give us commandments. He confirms this by stating that 'Communists preach absolutely no morals.'

# 2: Souls for Satan

When the Soviets in their early years adopted the slogan, 'Let us drive out the capitalists from earth and God from heaven', they were merely fulfilling the legacy of Karl Marx.

One of the peculiarities of black magic, as mentioned earlier, is the inversion of names. Inversions so permeated Marx's whole manner of thinking that he used them everywhere. He answered Proudhon's book *The Philosophy of Misery* with another book entitled *The Misery of Philosophy*. He also wrote, 'We have to use instead of the weapon of criticism, the criticism of weapons.'[31]

Here are some more examples of Marx's use of inversion in his writing:

'Let us seek the enigma of the Jew not in his religion, but rather let us seek the enigma of his religion in the real Jew.'[31a]

'Luther broke the faith in authority, because he restored the authority of faith. He changed the priests into laymen, because he changed the laymen into priests.'[31b]

Marx uses this technique in many places. He has what could be called the typical Satanist style.

Have you ever wondered about Marx's hair? Men usually wore beards in his time, but not beards like his, and they did not have long hair. Marx's manner of bearing himself was characteristic of the disciples of Joanna Southcott, a Satanic priestess who considered herself in contact with the demon Shiloh.[32] It is strange that some sixty years after her death in 1814, 'the Chatham group of Southcottians was joined by a soldier, James White, who, after his period of service in India, returned and took the lead

locally, developing further the doctrines of Joanna
. . . with a communistic tinge.'[33]

Marx did not often speak publicly about meta-
physics, but we can gather his views from the men
with whom he associated. One of his partners in the
First International was Mikhail Bakunin, a Russian
anarchist, who wrote:

'The Evil One is the satanic revolt against divine
authority, revolt in which we see the fecund germ of
all human emancipations, the revolution. Socialists
recognise each other by the words "In the name of
the one to whom a great wrong has been done."
Satan [is] the eternal rebel, the first freethinker and
the emancipator of worlds. He makes man ashamed
of his bestial ignorance and obedience; he emanci-
pates him, stamps upon his brow the seal of liberty
and humanity, in urging him to disobey and eat of
the fruit of knowledge.'[34]

Bakunin does more than praise Lucifer. He has a
concrete programme of revolution, but not one that
would free the poor from exploitation. He writes: 'In
this revolution we will have to awaken the devil in
the people, to stir up the basest passions. Our
mission is to destroy, not to edify. The passion of
destruction is a creative passion.'[35]

Karl Marx formed the First International together
with Bakunin and endorsed this strange programme.
Marx and Engels said in *The Communist Manifesto* that
the proletarian sees law, morality and religion as 'so
many bourgeois prejudices, behind which lurk in
ambush just as many bourgeois interests.'

Bakunin reveals that Proudhon, another major
Socialist thinker and at that time a friend of Karl
Marx, also 'worshipped Satan.'[36] Hess had introduced Marx to Proudhon, who wore the same hair
style typical of the nineteenth century Satanist sect
of Joanna Southcott.

Proudhon, in *The Philosophy of Misery*, declared that
God was the prototype for injustice. 'We reach

23

knowledge in spite of him, we reach society in spite of him. Every step forward is a victory in which we overcome the Divine.'[37]

He exclaims, 'Come, Satan, slandered by the small and by kings. God is stupidity and cowardice; God is hypocrisy and falsehood; God is tyranny and poverty; God is evil. Where humanity bows before an altar, humanity, the slave of kings and priests, will be condemned . . . I swear, God, with my hand stretched out towards the heavens, that you are nothing more than the executioner of my reason, the sceptre of my conscience . . . God is essentially anti-civilised, anti-liberal, anti-human.'[38] Proudhon declares God to be evil because man, his creation, is evil. Such thoughts are not original; they are the usual content of sermons in Satanist worship.

Marx later quarrelled with Proudhon and wrote a book to contradict his *Philosophy of Misery*. But Marx contradicted only minor economic doctrines. He had no objection to Proudhon's demonic anti-God rebellion.

Heinrich Heine, the renowned German poet, was a third intimate friend of Marx. He too was a Satan-fancier. He wrote:

> *I called the devil and he came,*
> *His face with wonder I must scan;*
> *He is not ugly, he is not lame.*
> *He is a delightful, charming man.*[39]

'Marx was a great admirer of Heinrich Heine . . . Their relationship was warm, hearty.'[39a]

Why should he have admired Heine? Perhaps for Satanist thoughts like the following: 'I have a desire . . . for a few beautiful trees before my door, and if dear God wishes to make me totally happy, he will give me the joy of seeing six or seven of my enemies hanged on these trees. With a compassionate heart I will forgive them after death all the wrong they have

24

done to me during their life. Yes, we must forgive our enemies, but not before they are hanged.

'I am not revengeful. I would like to love my enemies. But I cannot love them before taking revenge upon them. Only then my heart opens for them. As long as one has not avenged himself, bitterness remains in the heart.'

Would any decent man be an intimate friend of one who thinks like this?

Marx and his entourage thought alike. Lunatcharski, a leading philosopher who was once Minister of Education of the USSR, wrote in *Socialism and Religion* that Marx set aside all contact with God and instead put Satan in front of marching proletarian columns.

It is essential at this point to state emphatically that Marx and his comrades, while anti-God, were not atheists, as present-day Marxists claim to be. That is, while they openly denounced and reviled God, *they hated a God in whom they believed*. His existence is not challenged; His supremacy is.

When the revolution broke out in Paris in 1871, the Communard Flourens declared, 'Our enemy is God. Hatred of God is the beginning of wisdom.'[40]

Marx greatly praised the Communards who openly proclaimed this aim. But what has this to do with a more equitable distribution of goods or with better social institutions? Such are only the outward trappings for concealing the real aim—the total eradication of God and his worship. Today we see the evidence of this in such countries as Albania and North Korea, where all churches, mosques, and pagodas have been closed.


### Marx's Devilish Poetry

In Marx's poems *Invocation of One in Despair* and *Human Pride*, man's supreme supplication is for his

25

own greatness. If man is doomed to perish through his own greatness, this will be a cosmic catastrophe, but he will die as a godlike being, mourned by demons. Marx's ballad *The Player*, records the singer's complaints against a God who neither knows nor respects his art. It emerges from the dark abyss of hell, 'bedevilling the mind and bewitching the heart, and his dance is the dance of death.'[41] The minstrel draws his sword and throws it into the poet's soul.

'Art emerging from the dark abyss of hell, bedevilling the mind'. This reminds us of the words of the American revolutionist Jerry Rubin in *Do It:* 'We've combined youth, music, sex, drugs, and rebellion with treason—and that's a combination hard to beat.'[42]

In his poem *Human Pride*, Marx admits that his aim is not to improve the world, reform or revolutionise it, but simply to ruin it and to enjoy its being ruined:

> *With disdain I will throw my gauntlet*
> *Full in the face of the world,*
> *And see the collapse of this pygmy giant*
> *Whose fall will not stifle my ardour.*
>
> *Then will I wander godlike and victorious*
> *Through the ruins of the world*
> *And, giving my words an active force,*
> *I will feel equal to the Creator.*[43]

Marx adopted Satanism after an inner fight. The poems were ended in a period of severe illness, the result of this tempest within his heart. He writes at that time about his vexation at having to make an idol of a view he detests. He feels sick.[44]

The overriding reason for Marx's conversion to Communism appears clearly in a letter of his friend Georg Jung to Ruge: It is not the emancipation of the proletariat, nor the establishing of a better social order. Jung writes: 'If Marx, Bruno Bauer and Feuerbach associate to found a theological-political review, God would do well to surround himself with all his angels and indulge in self-pity, for these three will certainly drive him out of heaven . . .'[45]

Were these poems the only expressly Satanist writings of Karl Marx? We do not know, because the bulk of his works is kept secret by those who guard his manuscripts.

In *The Revolted Man*, Albert Camus wrote that thirty volumes of Marx and Engels have never been published and expressed the presumption that they are not much like what is generally known as Marxism.

On reading this, I had one of my secretaries write to the Marx-Lenin Institute in Moscow, asking if this assertion of the French writer is true.

I received a reply from the vice director, Professor M. Mtchedlov, who after saying Camus lied, confirmed his allegations. He further writes that there is no plan to complete the first edition of Marx and Engels. He says that of a total of 100 volumes, only thirteen have appeared. He offers a ridiculous excuse: World War II forestalled the printing of the other volumes. The letter was written in 1980, 35 years after the end of the war. And the State Publishing House of the Soviet Union surely has sufficient funds!

From this letter it is clear that though the Soviet Communists have all the manuscripts for 100 volumes, they have chosen to publish only thirteen. There is no other explanation than that most of Marx's ideas are intended to be kept secret.


## Marx's Ravaged Life

All active Satanists have ravaged personal lives. This was the case with Marx as well.

Arnold Künzli, in his book *Karl Marx—A Psycho-*

*gram*,[46] writes of Marx's life, which included the suicide of two daughters and a son-in-law. Three children died of malnutrition. His daughter Laura, married to the socialist Lafargue, also buried three of her children. Then she and her husband committed suicide together. Another daughter, Eleanor, decided with her husband to do likewise. She died; he backed out at the last minute.

Marx felt no obligation to earn a living for his family, though he could easily have done so, at least through his tremendous knowledge of languages. He lived by begging from Engels. He had an illegitimate child by his maidservant, Helen Demuth. Later he attributed the child to Engels, who accepted this comedy. He drank heavily. Riazanov, director of the Marx-Engels Institute in Moscow, admits this fact in his book *Karl Marx, Man, Thinker and Revolutionist*.[47]

Eleanor was Marx's favourite daughter. He called her Tussy and frequently said, 'Tussy is me.' She was shattered when she heard about the scandalous matter from Engels on his deathbed. It was this that led to her suicide.

It should be noted that Marx, in the *Communist Manifesto*, had railed against capitalists' 'having the wives and daughters of their proletarians at their disposal.'

There was an even darker spot in the life of Marx, the great revolutionary.

The German newspaper *Reichsruf* of 9 January 1960, published the fact that the Austrian Chancellor Raabe donated to Nikita Khrushchev, then dictator of Soviet Russia, an original letter of Karl Marx. Khrushchev did not enjoy it, because it was proof that Marx had been a paid informer of the Austrian police, spying on revolutionaries.

The letter had been found accidentally in a secret archive. It indicated that Marx the informer reported on his comrades during his exile in London. He received $25 for each bit of information he turned up. His notes were about the revolutionary exiles in London, Paris, and Switzerland.

One of those against whom he informed was Ruge, who considered himself an intimate friend of Marx. Letters in the language of a cordial relationship between the two still exist.

Rolv Heuer describes Marx's ravaged financial life in *Genius and Riches:* 'While he was a student in Berlin, the son of papa Marx received 700 thalers a year pocket-money.'[48] This was an enormous sum because at that time only five percent of the population had an annual income greater than 300 thalers. During his lifetime, Marx received from Engels some six million French francs (Figures from the Marx-Lenin Institute).

He always lusted after inheritances. While an uncle of his was in agony, Marx wrote, 'If the dog dies, I would be out of mischief.'[49] to which Engels answered, 'I congratulate you for the sickness of the hinderer of an inheritance, and I hope that the catastrophe will happen now.'[50]

Then 'the dog' died. Marx wrote, on 8 March 1855, 'A very happy event. Yesterday we were told about the death of the 90-year-old uncle of my wife. My wife will receive some 100 Lst; even more if the old dog has not left a part of his money to the lady who administered his house.'[51]

He did not have any kinder feelings to those who were much nearer to him than his uncle. He was not on speaking terms with his mother. In December 1863 he wrote to Engels, 'Two hours ago a telegram arrived to say that my mother is dead. Fate needed to take one member of the family. I already had one foot in the grave. Under the circumstances I am needed more than the old woman.

I have to go to Trier about their inheritance.'[52]

This was all he had to say at his mother's passing.

In addition, the relationship between Marx and his wife was demonstrably poor. She abandoned him

29

twice but returned each time. As for him, he did not even go to her funeral.

Always in need of funds, he lost much money at the stock exchange, where he, the economist, knew only how to lose.

Marx was an intellectual of high calibre. So was Engels. But their correspondence is full of obscenities, unusual in this class of society. Foul language abounds, and there is not one letter in which one hears an idealist speaking about his humanist or Socialist dream.

Since the Satanist sect is highly secret, we have only leads about the possibilities of Marx's connections with it. His disorderly life might be another link in the chain of evidence already considered.

## Engels' Counter-Conversion

Since Engels figures prominently in Marx's life, just a word about him. Engels had been brought up in a pietistic family. In his youth he had composed beautiful Christian poems. After meeting Marx, he wrote about him: 'Who is chasing with wild endeavour? A black man from Trier [Marx's birthplace], a remarkable monster. He does not walk or run, he jumps on his heels and rages full of anger as if he would like to catch the wide tent of the sky and throw it to the earth. He stretches his arms far away in the air; the wicked fist is clenched, he rages without ceasing, as if ten thousand devils had caught him by the hair.'[53]

Engels had begun to doubt the Christian faith after reading the book of a liberal theologian, Bruno Bauer. He had had a great struggle in his heart. He wrote at that time, 'I pray every day, indeed almost all day, for truth, and I have done so ever since I began to doubt, but still I cannot go back. My tears are welling as I write.'[54]

Engels did not find his way back to the Word of God, joining instead the one whom he himself had called 'the monster possessed by ten thousand devils.'[55] He had experienced a counterconversion.

What kind of person was Bruno Bauer, the liberal theologian who played a decisive role in the destruction of Engels' Christian faith and who endorsed Marx in his new anti-Christian ways? Did he have anything to do with demons?

Like Engels himself, he started life as a believer and later as a conservative theologian, who even wrote against critics of the Bible. Afterward, he himself became a radical critic of the Holy Scriptures and creator of a materialistic Christianity, which insisted that Jesus was only human, not the Son of God. Bauer wrote to his friend Arnold Ruge, also a friend of Marx and Engels, on 6 December, 1841:

'I deliver lectures here at the university before a large audience. I don't recognise myself when I pronounce my blasphemies from the pulpit. They are so great that these children, whom nobody should offend, have their hair standing on end. While delivering the blasphemies, I remember how I work piously at home writing an apology of the holy Scriptures and of the Revelation. In any case, it is a very bad demon that possesses me as often as I ascend the pulpit, and I am so weak that I am compelled to yield to him . . . My spirit of blasphemy will be satisfied only if I am authorised to preach openly as professor of the atheistic system.'[56]

The man who convinced Engels to become a Communist was the same Moses Hess who had previously convinced Marx. Hess writes, after meeting Engels in Cologne, 'He parted from me as an over-zealous Communist. This is how I produce ravages . . .'[57] To produce ravages—was this Hess's supreme purpose in life? It is Lucifer's, too.

The traces of having been a Christian never disappeared from Engels' mind. In 1865, he expresses his admiration for the song of the Reformation *A Mighty Fortress Is Our God*, calling it 'a triumphal hymn which became the Marseillaise of the 16th century.'[58] There are also other such pro-Christian sayings from his pen.

The tragedy of Engels is moving, even more gripping than that of Marx. Here is a wonderful Christian poem written in his youth by the man who would later become Marx's greatest accomplice in the destruction of religion;

> Lord Jesus Christ, God's only son,
> O step down from Thy heavenly throne
> And save my soul for me.
> Come down in all Thy blessedness,
> Light of Thy Father's holiness,
> Grant that I may choose Thee.
> Lovely, splendid, without sorrow is the joy
>     with which we raise,
> Saviour, unto Thee our praise.
>
> And when I draw my dying breath
> And must endure the pangs of death,
> Firm to Thee may I hold;
> That when my eyes with dark are filled
> And when my beating heart is stilled,
> In Thee shall I grow cold.
> Up in Heaven shall my spirit praise
>     Thy name eternally,
> Since it lies safe in Thee.
>
> O were the time of joy but nigh
> When from Thy loving bosom I
> Might draw new life that warms.
> And then, O God, with thanks to Thee,
> Shall I embrace those dear to me
> Forever in my arms.
> Ever, ever, ever-living,
> Thee abiding to behold
> Shall my life anew unfold.

*Thou camest Humankind to free*
*From death and ill, that there might be*
*Blessings and fortune everywhere.*
*And now with this, Thy new descent,*
*On Earth all shall be different;*
*To each man shalt Thou give his share.*[59]

After Bruno Bauer had sown doubts in his soul, Engels wrote to some friends, 'It is written, "Ask and it shall be given unto you." I seek truth wherever I have the hope of finding at least a shadow of it. Still I cannot recognise your truth as the eternal truth. Yet it is written, "Seek and ye shall find. Who is the man among you who would give to his child a stone, when it asks for bread? Even less will your Father who is in heaven."

'Tears come into my eyes while I write this. I am moved through and through, but I feel I will not be lost. I will come to God, after whom my whole soul longs. This, too, is a witness of the Holy Spirit. With this I live and with this I die . . . The Spirit of God witnesses to me, that I am a child of God.'[60]

Engels was very well aware of the Satanist danger.

In his book *Schelling, Philosopher in Christ*, Engels wrote: 'Since the terrible French Revolution, an entirely new, devilish spirit has entered into a great part of mankind, and godlessness lifts its daring head in such an unashamed and subtle manner that you would think the prophecies of Scripture are fulfilled now. Let us see first what the Scriptures say about the godlessness of the last times. The Lord Jesus says in Matthew 24:11–13 "Many false prophets shall rise, and shall deceive many. And because iniquity shall abound, the love of many shall wax cold. But he that shall endure unto the end, the same shall be saved. And this gospel of the kingdom shall be preached in all the world for a witness unto all nations; and then shall the end come." And then in v. 24 "There shall arise Christs, and false prophets, and shall show great signs and wonders; insomuch that, if it were possible, they shall deceive the very elect." And St. Paul says, in 2 Thessalonians 2:3ff "That man of sin shall be revealed, the son of perdition, who opposes and exalts himself above all that is God, or that is worshipped . . . [The coming of the Wicked] is after the working of Satan with all power and signs and lying wonders, and with all deceivableness of unrighteousness in them that perish; because they received not the love of the truth, that they might be saved. And for this cause God shall send them strong delusion, that they should believe a lie: that they all might be damned who believed not the truth, but had pleasure in unrighteousness." ' Engels quotes Scripture after Scripture just as the most Bible-believing theologian would do.

He continues: 'We have nothing to do any more with indifference or coldness toward the Lord. No, it is an open, declared enmity, and in the place of all sects and parties we have now only two: Christians and anti-Christians . . . We see the false prophets among us . . . They travel throughout Germany and wish to intrude everywhere; they teach their Satanic teachings in the market-places and bear the flag of the devil from one town to another, seducing the poor youth, in order to throw them in the deepest abyss of hell and death.' He finishes this book with the words of Revelation: 'Behold, I come soon. Keep what you have, that nobody take away from you your crown. Amen.'[61]

The man who wrote such poems and such warnings against Satanism, the man who prayed with tears to beware of this danger, the man who recognised Marx as being possessed with a thousand devils, becomes Marx's closest collaborator in the devilish fight, 'for Communism abolishes eternal truths, it abolishes all religion, and all morality . . .'[62]

Liberal theology had accomplished this monstrous change. It shares with Marx and Engels the guilt for the tens of millions of innocents killed by Communism.

## Marx Hates Whole Nations

Marx's whole attitude and conversation were satanic in nature. Though a Jew, he wrote a pernicious anti-Jewish book called *The Jewish Question*.

In 1856, he wrote in *The New York Tribune* an article entitled 'The Russian Loan', in which we read: 'We know that behind every tyrant stands a Jew, as a Jesuit stands behind every Pope. As the army of the Jesuits kills every free thought, so the desire of the oppressed would have chances of success, the usefulness of wars incited by capitalists would cease, if it were not for the Jews who steal the treasures of mankind. It is no wonder that 1856 years ago Jesus chased the usurers from the Jerusalem temple. They were like the contemporary usurers who stand behind tyrants and tyrannies. The majority of them are Jewish. The fact that the Jews have become so strong as to endanger the life of the world causes us to disclose their organisation, their purpose, that its stench might awaken the workers of the world to fight and eliminate such a canker.' Did Hitler say anything worse than this?

Strangely, Marx also wrote to the contrary, in *The Capital*, Vol. I, under the heading 'The Capitalist Character of Manufacture': 'In the front of the chosen people it was written that they are the property of Jehovah.'

Many other Jewish Communists imitated Marx in their hatred of Jews.

Ruth Fisher, renowned German Jewish Communist leader and a member of Parliament, said: 'Squash the Jewish capitalists, hang them from the lamp posts; tread them under your feet.'[63]

Why just the Jewish capitalists and not the others remains an unanswered question.

Marx hated not only the Jews but also the Germans: "Beating is the only means of resurrecting the Germans.' He spoke about 'the stupid German people. . . . the disgusting national narrowness of the Germans' and said that 'Germans, Chinese, and Jews have to be compared with peddlers and small merchants.'[64] He called the Russians 'cabbage-eaters.'[65] The Slavic peoples are 'ethnic trash.'[66] He expressed his hatred of many nations, but never his love.

Marx wrote in his new year's round-up of 1848 about 'the Slavic riff-raff', which included Russians, Czechs and Croats. These 'retrograde' races had nothing left for them by fate except 'the immediate task of perishing in the revolutionary world storm.' 'The coming world war will cause not only reactionary classes and dynasties, but entire reactionary peoples, to disappear from the face of the earth. And that will be progress.' 'Their very name will vanish.'[67]

Neither Marx nor Engels were concerned about the destruction of millions of people. The former wrote, 'A silent, unavoidable revolution is taking place in society, a revolution that cares as little about the human lives it destroys as an earthquake cares about the houses it ravages. Classes and races that are too weak to dominate the new conditions of existence will be defeated.'

By way of contrast, Hitler, who desired only the enslavement, not the destruction, of these nations, was much more humane than Marx.

Engels wrote in the same vein: 'The next world war will make whole reactionary peoples disappear from the face of the earth. This, too, is progress.'[68] 'Obviously this cannot be fulfilled without crushing some delicate national flower. But without violence and without pitilessness nothing can be obtained in history.'[68a]

Marx, the man who posed as a forefighter for the proletariat, called this class of people 'stupid boys, rogues, asses.'

Engels well knew what to expect from them. He wrote, 'The democtratic, red, yes, even the Communist mob, will never love us.'

Marx identified black people with 'idiots' and constantly used the offensive term 'nigger' in private correspondence.

He called his rival Lassalle 'the Jewish nigger' and made it very clear that this was not intended as an epithet of disdain for just one person. 'It is now absolutely clear to me that, as both the shape of his head and his hair texture shows, he is descended from the Negroes who joined Moses' flight from Egypt (unless his mother or grandmother on the paternal side hybridised with a nigger) . . . The pushiness of the fellow is also nigger-like.'

Marx even championed slavery in North America. For this, he quarrelled with his friend Proudhon, who had advocated the emancipation of slaves in the U.S. He wrote in response, 'Without slavery, North America, the most progressive of countries, would be transformed into a patriarchal country. Wipe North America from the map of the world and you will have anarchy—the complete decay of modern commerce and civilisation. Abolish slavery and you will have wiped America off the map of nations.'[69]

Marx also wrote, 'The devil take the British'.[70]

In spite of such propositions, there are plenty of British, as well as American Marxists.

## Satan Is in the Family

Marx's favourite daughter Eleanor, with her father's approval, married Edward Aveling. He lectured on subjects such as 'The Wickedness of God' (exactly as Satanists do; unlike atheists, they do not deny the existence of God, except to deceive others; they know of His existence but describe Him as wicked). In his lectures he tried to prove that God is 'an encourager of polygamy and an instigator to theft.' He advocated the right to blaspheme.[71]

Marx's chosen son-in-law was a lecturer in this movement. The following poem describes the attitudes of his circle toward Satanism:

> To thee my verses, unbridled and daring,
> Shall mount, O Satan, king of the banquet.
> Away with thy sprinkling, O priest, and
>     thy droning,
> For never shall Satan, O priest, stand
>     behind thee.
>
> Thy breath, O Satan, my verses inspires,
> When from my bosom the gods I defy.
> Of kings pontifical, of kings inhuman:
> Thine is the lightning that sets minds
>     to shaking.
>
> O soul that wanderest far from the
>     straight way,
> Satan is merciful. See Heloisa!
>
> Like the whirlwind spreading its wings,
> He passes, O people, Satan the great!
> Hail, of reason the great Vindicator!
> Sacred to thee shall rise incense and vows!
> Thou hast the god of the priest
>     disenthroned[72]

## A Housemaid's Revelation

An American, Commander Sergius Riis, had been a disciple of Marx. Grieved by the news of his death, he went to London to visit the house in which the admired teacher had lived. The family had moved. The only one whom he could interview was Marx's former housemaid Helen Demuth. She said these amazing words about him: 'He was a God-fearing man. When very sick, he prayed alone in his room before a row of lighted candles, tying a sort of tape measure around his forehead.'[73] This suggests philacteries, implements worn by Orthodox Jews during their morning prayers.

But Marx had been baptised in the Christian religion. He had never practised Judaism. He later became a fighter against God. He wrote books against religion and he brought up all his children as atheists. What was this ceremony that an ignorant maid considered a prayer? Jews when saying their prayers with philacteries on their forehead usually don't have a row of candles before them. Could this have been some magic practice?

We also know that Marx, the presumed atheist, had in his study a bust of Zeus. In Greek mythology, Zeus, a cruel heathen deity, transformed himself into a beast and took Europe captive—exactly what Marxism did later. The naked figure of Zeus, known for his ferocity, is also the only religious emblem in the main lobby of the Organisation of United Nations in New York.

## Family Letters

Another possible hint is contained in a letter written to Marx by his son Edgar on 31 March 1854. It begins with the startling words, 'My dear devil.'[74] Who has ever known of a son addressing his father like this? Yet that is how a Satanist writes to his beloved one. Could the son have been initiated too?

It is no less significant that Marx's wife addresses him as follows, in a letter of August 1844: 'Your last pastoral letter, high priest and bishop of souls, has

39

again given quiet rest and peace to your poor sheep.'[75]

Marx had expressed his desire in *The Communist Manifesto* to abolish all religion, which one might assume would include abolishing the Satanist cult too. Yet his wife refers to him as high priest and bishop. Of what religion? The only European religion with high priests is the Satanist one. What pastoral letters did he, the man believed to have been an atheist, write? Where are they? There is a part of Marx's life which has remained unresearched.

## Biographers' Testimonies

Some biographers of Marx might have had an intuition about the connection between devil-worship and the subject of their book, but not having the necessary spiritual preparation they could not understand the facts they had before their eyes. Still their testimony is interesting.

The Marxist Franz Mehring wrote in his book *Karl Marx*: 'Although Karl Marx's father died a few days after his son's twentieth birthday, he seems to have observed with secret apprehension the demon in his favourite son . . . [76] Henry Marx did not think and could not have thought that the rich store of bourgeois culture which he handed on to his son Karl as a valuable heritage for life would only help to deliver the demon he feared.'[77]

Marx died in despair, as all Satanists do. On 25 May 1883, he wrote to Engels, 'How pointless and empty is life, but how desirable!'[78]

Marx was a contemporary of great Christians: the composer Mendelssohn, the philanthropist Dr Barnardo, the preachers Charles Spurgeon and General William Booth. All lived near him in London. He never mentions them. They went unobserved.

There is a secret behind Marx which only a very

few Marxists know. Lenin wrote, 'After half a century, not one of the Marxists has comprehended Marx.'[79]


## The Secret Behind Lenin's Life

There is a secret behind Lenin's life too.

When I wrote the first edition of the present book, I knew of no personal involvement of Lenin with any rituals of the Satanist sect. Since then, I have read *The Young Lenin* by Trotsky, who was Lenin's intimate friend and co-worker. He writes that Lenin, at the age of 16, tore the cross from his neck, spat on it, and trod it underfoot, a very common Satanist ceremony.

There is not the slightest doubt that he was dominated by Satanist ideology. How else could one explain the following quotation from his letter to the Russian writer Maxim Gorki, dated 13–14 November 1913:

'Millions of sins, mischiefs, oppressions, and physical epidemics, are more easily discovered by the people, and therefore less dangerous, than the thinnest idea of a spiritual little god, even if disguised in the most decorous garb?'[80]

In the end, Satan deceived him, as he does all his followers.

Lenin was moved to write as follows about the Soviet state:

'The State does not function as we desired. How does it function? The car does not obey. A man is at the wheel and seems to lead it, but the car does not drive in the desired direction. It moves as another force wishes.'[81]

What is this other mysterious force which supersedes even the plans of the Bolshevik leaders? Did they sell out to a force which they hoped to master but which proved more powerful than even they anticipated and drove them to despair?

In a letter of 1921 Lenin wrote: 'I hope we will be hanged on a stinking rope. And I did not lose the hope that this would happen, because we cannot condemn this dirty bureaucracy. If this happens, it will be well done.'[82]

This was Lenin's last hope after a whole life of struggle for the Communist cause: to be justly hanged on a stinking rope. This hope was not fulfilled in his life, but almost all of his co-workers were eventually executed by Stalin after having confessed publicly that they had served other powers than the proletariat they pretended to help.

What a confession from Lenin: 'I hope we will be hanged on a stinking rope'!

It is interesting to note that at the age of 13 Lenin wrote what could be called prophetic poetry foretelling the bankruptcy with which his life would end. He had decided to serve mankind, but without God. These were his words:

*Sacrificing your life freely for others,*
*It is a pity you will have the sad fate*
*That your sacrifice will be completely fruitless.*[83]

What a contrast to the words of another fighter, St Paul the apostle, who wrote towards the end of his life: 'I have fought the good fight, I have finished my course . . . Henceforth there is laid up for me a crown of righteousness, which the Lord, the righteous judge, shall give me at that day' (II Timothy 4:7,8).

There exists a 'too late.' Esau repented with many tears for having sold his birthright, but the deal could not be undone.

Lenin, founder of the Soviet state, said on his deathbed, 'I committed a great error. My nightmare is to have the feeling that I'm lost in an ocean of blood from the innumerable victims. It is too late to return. To save our country, Russia, we would have needed men like Francis of Assisi. With ten men like him we would have saved Russia.'

## Bukharin, Stalin, Mao, Ceaushescu, Andropov

It might be instructive at this point to take a look at some modern Marxists. Bukharin, secretary general of the Communist International and one of the chief Marxist doctrinaires in this century, knew as early as the age of twelve, after reading the book of Revelation in the Bible, that he longed to become the Antichrist. Realising from Scripture that the Antichrist had to be the son of the apocalyptic great whore, he insisted that his mother confess to having been a harlot.

About Stalin he wrote, 'He is not a man, but a devil.'[84]

Too late Bukharin realised into whose hands he had fallen. In a letter which he made his wife memorise just before his arrest and execution, he said: 'I am leaving life. I am lowering my head . . . I feel my helplessness before a hellish machine . . .'[85] He had helped erect a guillotine—the Soviet State—that had killed millions, only to learn in the end that its design had been made in hell. He had desired to be the Antichrist. He became instead its victim.

Kaganovitch, Stalin's brother-in-law and closest collaborator, writes about him in his Diary:

'I started to understand how Stalin managed to make himself a god. He did not have a single human characteristic . . . Even when he exhibited some emotions, they all did not seem to belong to him. They were as false as the scale on top of armour. And behind this scale was Stalin himself—a piece of steel. For some reason I was convinced that he would live forever . . . He was not human at all.'

'Rosa [his wife] says he makes her climb a tree wearing nothing but stockings. I have a feeling he is not human at all. He is too unusual to be a regular human being. Although he looks like an ordinary man. Such a puzzle. What is it I'm writing? Am I raving mad, too?'

Stalin described to Kaganovitch his spiritual exercises. Believers of various religions engage in the practice of meditation on what is beautiful, wise and good, to help them become more loving. Stalin indulged in just the opposite practice.

He told Kaganovitch: 'When I have to say good-bye to someone, I picture this person on all fours and he becomes disgusting. Sometimes I feel attached to a person who should be removed for the good of the cause. What do you think I do? I imagine this person shitting, exhaling stench, farting, vomiting and I don't feel sorry for this person. The sooner he stops stinking on this earth, the better. And I cross this person out of my heart.'

One of Stalin's amusements was to put green glasses on the eyes of horses to make them see hay as grass. He also put dark glasses of atheism on the eyes of men to keep them from seeing God's green pastures, reserved for believing souls.

The Diary contains many revealing insights. 'Many times Stalin spoke of religion as our most vicious enemy. He hates religion for many reasons, and I share his feelings. Religion is a cunning and dangerous enemy . . . Stalin also thinks that separation from children should be the main punishment for all parents belonging to sects, irrespective of whether they were convicted or not.

'I think he secretly engaged in astrology. One peculiar feature of his always astonished me. He always talked with some veiled respect about God and religion. At first, I thought I was imagining it, but gradually I realised it was true. But he was always careful when the subject came up. And I was never able to find out exactly what his point of view was. One thing became very clear to me—his treatment of God and religion was very special. For example, he never said directly there was no God . . .

'People ceased somehow to be their own selves in his presence. They all admired him and worshipped him. I don't think he enjoyed any great love of the nation: he was above it. It may sound strange but he occupied a position previously reserved only for God.'

It belongs to the tragedy of human existence that one has enemies and is sometimes obliged to fight them. Marx took delight in this sad necessity. His favourite verse, which he often repeated, was, 'There is nothing more beautiful in the world than to bite one's enemies.'[85a]

No wonder his follower Stalin said that the greatest joy is to cultivate a person's friendship until he lays his head confidently on your bosom, then to implant a dagger in his back; it is a pleasure not to be surpassed.[85b]

Marx had expressed the same idea long before. He wrote to Engels about comrades with whom he disagreed: 'We must make these rogues believe that we continue our relationship with them, until we have the power to sweep them away from our road, in one manner or another.'[85c]

It is significant that many of Stalin's comrades-in-arms speak about him as demonic.

Milovan Djilas, prominent Communist leader of Yugoslavia who was personally well acquainted with Stalin, wrote: 'Was it not so that the demonic power and energy of Stalin consisted in this, that he made the [Communist] movement and every person in it pass to a state of confusion and stupefaction, thus creating and ensuring his reign of fear . . . ?'[86]

He also says about the whole ruling class of the U.S.S.R. 'They make a semblance of believing in the ideal of Socialism, in a future society without classes.

45

In reality, they believe in nothing except organised power.'[87]

Even Stalin's daughter, Svetlana Alliluyeva, who never learned about the depths of Satanism, wrote, 'Beria (the Soviet minister of Interior Affairs) seems to have had a diabolic link with all our family . . . Beria was a frightening, wicked demon . . . A terrible demon had taken possession of my father's soul.' Svetlana further mentions that Stalin considered goodness and all-forgiving love to be worse than the greatest crime.[88]

Such is the Satanic priesthood that rules almost half of mankind, and which orders terrorist acts all over the world.

It is only fair to add a few words that might serve to explain the essence of the man Stalin.

He was the illegitimate child of a landlord by a servant-maid. His father, fearing notoriety, bribed a cobbler to marry the pregnant girl, but the affair became known. During his childhood, Stalin was mocked as a bastard. When he was a teenager, his real father was found murdered. Stalin was suspected, but no proof could be found against him.

Later, as a seminary student, he joined Communist circles. There he fell in love with a girl named Galina. Since the Communists were poor, Galina was given the assignment to become the mistress of a rich man and so provide the Party with money. When Stalin voted for this proposal, she cut her veins. She had loved Stalin.

He himself received from the Party the assignment to commit robberies, and in this he was very successful. He appropriated none of the stolen money for himself.

He was also assigned the duty of infiltrating the Czarist police. He had to play the dual role of their informer, denouncing some unimportant Party members, in order to find out secrets of the police and protect the important Communists.

As a young man, therefore, Stalin had the worst possible heredity, education, and development. Thus he was easily susceptible to Satanist influence. He became what his pseudonym 'Stalin' means: a man of steel, without the slightest human emotion or pity.

(Andropov, late premier of the Soviets, produced the same impression as Stalin. The French Minister of External Affairs Claude Cheysson, who met him, described Andropov in *Le Monde*, Paris, as 'a man without warmth of soul, who works like a computer . . . He shows no emotions . . . He is extremely dispassionate . . . He is accurate in words and gestures like a computer').

Stalin, like Marx, Engels and Bauer before him, started out as a believer. At 15, he wrote his first poem, which begins with the words, 'Great is the Almighty's providence.' He became a seminarian because he felt it his calling.[89] There he became first a Darwinist, then a Marxist.

When he began to write as a revolutionary, the first pseudonyms he used were 'Demonoshvili',[90] meaning something like 'the demoniac' in the Georgian language, and 'Besoshvili',[91] 'the devilish.'

Troitskaia, daughter of the Soviet marshal Tuhatchevsky, one of the top men of the Red Army, later shot by Stalin, wrote about her father that he had a picture of Satan in the east corner of his bedroom, where the Orthodox usually put their ikons.

In Czechoslovakia, when a Communist was named head of the State Council for Religious Affairs, an institution whose purpose is to spy on believers and persecute them, he took the name 'Hruza', which means in Slovak 'horror', an appellation used for 'devil.'

One of the leaders of a terrorist organisation in Argentina took the nickname 'Satanovsky.'

Anatole France was a renowned French Communist writer who introduced some of the greatest intellectuals of France to Communism. At a recent exhibition of demoniac art in Paris, one of the pieces shown was the specific chair used by the Communist writer for presiding over Satanist rituals. It's horned arm rests and legs were covered with goats's fur.[92]

Britain's centre of Satanism is Highgate Cemetery in London, where Karl Marx is buried. Mysterious rites of black magic are celebrated at this tomb.[93] It was the place of inspiration for the Highgate Vampire who attacked girls in 1970.[94] Hua-Kuo-Feng, dictator of Red China, also paid it his respects.

Ulrike Meinhof, Eselin, and other German Red terrorists have been involved in the occult.[95]

One of the oldest devil-worshipping sects, the Syrian Yezidi, is described in a Soviet atheistic magazine, *Nauka I Religia* (July 1979). It is the only religious sect about which the magazine wrote not the slightest word of criticism.

As for Mao-Tse-Tung, he wrote: 'From the age of eight I hated Confucius. In our village there was a Confucianist temple. With all my heart, I wished only one thing: to destroy it to its very foundations.'[96]

Is it normal for a child at the age of eight to wish only the destruction of his own religion? Such thoughts belong to demonic characters.

Again at the other extreme, there is St. Paul of the Cross, who from the age of eight spent three hours in prayer every night.

## Cult of Violence

Engels wrote in *Anti-Duhring*, 'Universal love for men is an absurdity.' And in a letter to a friend he said, 'We need hate rather than love—at least for now.'

Che Guevara learned his lessons well; in his writings he echoes Engels' sentiments: 'Hate is an element of fight—pitiless hate against the foe, hate that lifts the revolutionist above the natural limitation of man and makes him become an efficient, destructive, cool, calculating, and cold killing machine.'

This is what the devil wishes to make of men. He has succeeded all too well with many notorious leaders of the human race. In our lifetime we have witnessed more than our share: Hitler, Eichmann, Mengell, Stalin, Mao, Andropov, Pol Pot.

Marx writes in *The Communist Manifesto*: 'The Communists despise making a secret of their opinions and intentions. They openly declare that their aims can be reached only through the violent overthrow of the whole existing social structure.' Further: 'There is only one method to shorten the murderous pains of death of the old society, the bloody birth pangs of the new society; only one method to simplify and concentrate them, that is revolutionary terrorism.'[96a]

There have been many revolutions in history. Each had an objective: the American revolution was fought for national independence, the French revolution for democracy. Marx is the only one who formulates as his aim a 'permanent revolution', terrorism and bloodshed for revolution's sake. There is no purpose to be attained. Violence to the point of paroxysm is its only objective. This is what distinguishes Satanism from ordinary human sinfulness.

Terrorists executed in Czarist Russia for murder he called 'immortal martyrs' or 'amazingly capable fellows.'[96b]

Engels wrote, too, of the 'bloody revenge we take.' This expression occurs often. 'In the interior, [of Russia], what a splendid development. The attempts at murder become frequent.' 'Leaving aside the problem of morality . . . for a revolutionist any means are right which lead to the purpose, the violent, as the seemingly tame.'[96c]

The Marxist Lenin, while living under the democratic rule of Kerensky in Russia, said, 'What is needed is wild energy and again energy. I wonder, yea more, I am horrified that more than half a year has passed in speaking about bombs and not one single bomb has been fabricated.'[96d]

A further insight into the fundamental attitudes of Communists can be gained from a few brief quotes:

Marx: 'We make war against all prevailing ideas of religion, of the state, of country, of patriotism. The idea of God is the keynote of a perverted civilisation. It must be destroyed.'

Lenin: 'We have to use any ruse, dodge, trick, cunning, unlawful method, concealment, and veiling of the truth. The basic rule is to exploit the conflicting interests of the capitalist states.'

Communist Manifesto: 'The Communists disdain to conceal their views and aims. They openly declare that their aims can be attained only by the forcible overthrow of all the existing social conditions. Let the ruling class tremble at a Communist revolution.'

Lenin: 'Atheism is an integral part of Marxism. Marxism is materialism. We must combat religion. This is the ABC of all materialism and consequently of Marxism.'

Lenin in an address in 1922: 'First we shall take Eastern Europe, then the masses of Asia. After that, we shall surround and undermine the U.S.A., which will fall into our hands without a struggle—like an overripe fruit.'

Khruschev: 'If anyone believes our smiles involve abandonment of the teachings of Marx, Engels and Lenin, he deceives himself. Those who wait for that must wait until a shrimp learns to whistle.'

## Satanist Cruelty

Solzhenitsyn reveals in his monumental Gulag Archipelago[97] that the hobby of Yagoda, the Soviet Union's minister of Interior Affairs, was to undress and, naked, to shoot at images of Jesus and the saints. A couple of comrades joined him at this. Another Satanist ritual practised in Communist high places!

Why should men allegedly representing the proletariat shoot at the image of Jesus, a proletarian, or of the virgin Mary, a poor woman?

The Pentecostals recall an incident that took place in Russia during World War II. One of their preachers had exorcised a devil who threatened, upon leaving the possessed, 'I will take revenge.' Several years later the Pentecostal preacher who had performed the exorcism was shot for his faith. The officer who executed him said just before pulling the trigger, 'Now we are even.'

Are Communist officers sometimes possessed by devils? Do they perhaps serve as Satan's instruments of revenge against Christians who seek to overthrow his throne?

In Russia in Stalin's day, some Communists killed a number of innocents in the cellars of the police. After their bloody deed, one of the henchmen had second thoughts and went from corpse to corpse, apologising: 'I did not intend to do this. I don't know you. Speak to me, move, forgive me.' One of his comrades killed him. A third was converted and related the incident.

*Russkaia Misl*, a Russian-language magazine appearing in France, reported on 13 March 1975, the following from the Soviet Union:

D. Profirevitch, in Russia, had a daughter and a son whom he brought up in the faith. Naturally, they had to attend Communist schools. At the age of twelve the daughter came home and told her parents, 'Religion is a capitalist superstition. We are living in new times.' She dropped Christianity altogether. Afterwards she joined the Communist Party and became a member of the Secret Police. This was a terrible blow to her parents.

Later on the mother was arrested. Under Communist rule no one possesses anything, whether it be children, a wife, or personal liberty. The State can take them away at any time.

After the mother's arrest the son exhibited great sorrow. A year later, he hanged himself. D. Profirevitch found this suicide letter: 'Father, will you judge me? I am a member of the Communist youth organisation. I had to sign that I would report everything to the Soviet authorities. One day the police called me, and Varia, my sister, asked me to sign a denunciation against mother because as a Christian she is considered a counterrevolutionist. I signed. I am guilty of her imprisonment. Now they have ordered me to spy on you. The consequence will be the same. Forgive me, father; I have decided to die.' The suicide of the son was followed by the jailing of the father.[98]

Father Kovalyk was arrested by the Bolsheviks in the year 1941 and was confined in the Brygidka jail in Lviv, Ukraine. When the Germans put the Bolsheviks to flight that same year, the people of the city found the priest's blood-stained body nailed to the wall by the arms and legs, as if it were the crucified Lord. They also found about six thousand massacred prisoners, shot in the nape of the neck, whom the Bolsheviks had piled on top of each other in the cellars and covered over with plaster.

Dr O. Sas-Yavorsky (U.S.A.), after the capture of Lviv by the Germans near the end of June 1941, went searching for his imprisoned father and saw in the jail a priest nailed to the cross. Into his slashed stomach the NKVD had placed the body of an as yet unborn baby, taken from the womb of its mother, whose mutilated dead body lay on the blood-soaked floor.

Other eyewitnesses recognised that this was the body of the renowned missionary Father Zynoviy Kovalyk, C.S.S.R.[99]

Generally, to the Communists human life is cheap. Lenin wrote during the civil war. 'It would be a shame not to shoot men for not obeying the draft and avoiding mobilisation. Report more often about the results.'[100]

During the Spanish civil war, the Communists killed 4,000 Catholic priests.

The renowned Russian Orthodox priest Dudko reported that six Communists entered the house of Father Nicholas Tchardjov, pulled out his hair, gouged out his eyes, made many cuts on his body, passed a pressing iron over it, then shot him with two bullets.

This happened on the Eve of St. Nicholas. It was not only a crime against the priest but also a mockery of the saint.

The Western press reported on 10 March 1983, that in Zimbabwe 3,000 of the Ndebele tribe were killed by the soldiers of the Communist dictator Mugabe. The army had been trained by North Korean instructors. Tribe members were asked to shoot their grown-up sons themselves; if they refused, they were shot together with their sons.

Marxism promises a paradise on earth.

Well, the devil is God's monkey. He apes God by promising still waters and green pastures, which are not his to give. Therefore he must pretend. And the less he can offer, the more he must pretend. To gain a foothold, he puts on a false front (did you ever wonder about Communist front organisations?) and makes benevolent gestures.

But he delivers only misery, death, and destruction 'awful, complete, universal, and pitiless.'

The devil is jealous and becomes enraged at spiritual beauty. It offends him. If he cannot be beautiful—and he lost his primal beauty because of his pride—he does not want anyone else to be. If it were not for the saints' spiritual beauty, the devil would not seem so ugly. Therefore he wishes to deface all beauty.

For this reason, Christians in the Romanian Communist prison of Piteshti, as well as other

Communist jails, were tortured not only to betray the secrets of the Underground church, but also to blaspheme.

Regimes under which such horrors occur again and again, regimes that turn even Christians into murderers and denouncers of innocent victims, can only be abhorred by the children of God. Whoever bids them Godspeed is a partaker of their evil deeds (2 John 11).

# 3: Satan and Marx Worldwide

I have written that Marxism is satanic. But is not every sin satanic by its very nature? Can there exist satanic and non-satanic sin?

I pondered long about this. Then I had a dream one night that clarified my thinking.

In my dream I saw a prostitute hooking young men who were just leaving church. I asked her, 'Why did you choose this particular place to work?'

She replied, 'My delight is to lead young men into sin just as they come from worship. The Greek word for worship in the New Testament is *proskun*, which means etymologically "to kiss." The worshipper stepping out of the house of prayer still has the imprint of Jesus' kisses on his mouth. What a satisfaction to defile him just then, to make him wallow in the bed of lasciviousness and then say to him, "You see, Jesus to whom you prayed could not keep you from sin for even five minutes. He is not the Saviour. My master is more powerful than He." '

Sexual impurity is a common human sin. But Mephistopheles asks Faust to seduce Gretchen just as she is walking to church with a prayer book in her hand. This is satanic. It is also satanic to plan the seduction of a clergyman and to perform the act in a church.

To write, read, or view pornography is another common sin. But it is a characteristic of American pornography, which promotes incest, pederasty, and perversions, that it is full of the names of God, Christ, and Mary. With every obscenity there is a sacred word, with every ugly gesture a heavenly expression, to defile and profane the holy. This is satanic.

To crucify the innocent is a very common sin. To

crucify Jesus, the Son of God, between two thieves to suggest guilt by association is satanic.

To kill political enemies, to make war and stir up revolution—even with mass killings—is human sinfulness. But the Russian Communists, after having killed millions of their enemies, turned their violence against their friends, including even their most illustrious comrades, the chief perpetrators of their revolution. This is the seal of Satanism. It is revolution not for attaining a goal, but revolution and killing for killing's sake, what Marx called 'the permanent revolution.'

Of 29 members and candidates in the Central Committee of the Soviet Communists in 1917, year of the revolution, only four had the good fortune to depart this life before being deprived of it. One of the four was posthumously declared 'an enemy of the revolution.'

Thirteen were sentenced to death by their own comrades or disappeared. Two were so persecuted by Stalin that they committed suicide.[101]

To be a criminal or a mafiosi is a heinous human sin, but the satanic goes beyond even what the Mafia allows.

Tomasso Buscetta, one of the representative figures of the Sicilian Mafia, who became a police informer and revealed the crimes of this organisation, said: 'Crime is a necessity that one cannot avoid, but that always has a reason. With us gratuitous crime, which is an end in itself or the result of an individual impulse, is excluded. We exclude, for example, "transversal vendetta", i.e., the calculated killing of someone near the target of our crime, such as a wife, children, or relatives.'

Satanic crime is of another order. Hitler killed millions of Jews, including babies, with the excuse that some Jews had done harm to the German people. For the Communists it was a matter of course

56

to imprison and torture the family members of a person they considered guilty.

When I was jailed, it was taken for granted that my wife must be jailed, too, and my son must be excluded from all schooling.

Marxism is not an ordinary sinful human ideology. It is satanic in its manner of sinning, as it is satanic in the teachings it purveys. In certain circumstances, it openly avowed its satanic character.

One can judge a teacher by his disciples. To give just one example: Consider this dictum of the painter Picasso: 'An artist must discover the way to convince his public of the full truth of his lies.'[102]

Who was the man who wrote this monstrosity? It was the same one who wrote, 'I came to Communism as one comes to a fountain . . . My adherence to Communism is the logical consequence of my entire life and work.'[103]

One becomes a Marxist because his ideal is a lie.

To gain an insight into the life and thinking of a key Satanist, one need only read a few mild excerpts from the writings of Aleister Crowley (1875–1947), notorious for his involvement in occult practices:

'Pity not the fallen. I never knew them. I console not. I hate the consoler and the consoled.'[104]

'The wolf betrays only the greedy and treacherous, the raven betrays only the melancholy and dishonest. But I am he of whom it is written: He shall deceive the very elect . . .

'I have feasted myself on the blood of the saints, but I am not suspected of men to be their enemy, for my fleece is white and warm, for my teeth are not the teeth of one that tears flesh, and my eyes are mild, and they know me not as the chief of the lying spirits . . .'[105]

'Beautiful art thou, O Babylon, and desirable . . . O Babylon, Babylon, thou mighty mother, that ride upon the crowned beasts, let me be drunken upon the wine of your fornication; let your kisses wanton me unto death.'[106]

Crowley quotes a multitude of sayings like this from completely unknown older Satanist works, unavailable to the uninitiated.


## Blasphemous Versions of the Lord's Prayer

The Soviet newspaper *Soviestskaia Molodioj*, of 14 February 1976, adds a new and shattering proof of the connections between Marxism and Satanism. It describes how the militant Communists stormed churches and mocked God under the Czarist regime. For this purpose the Communists used a blasphemous version of the 'Our Father':

> *Our father, which art in Petersburg*
> *[today, Leningrad],*
> *Cursed be your name,*
> *May your Kingdom crumble,*
> *May your will not be fulfilled,*
> *yea, not even in hell.*
> *Give us our bread which you stole from us,*
> *And pay our debts, as we paid yours until now,*
> *And don't lead us further into temptation*
> *But deliver us from evil—the police of Plehve*
> *[the Czarist prime minister],*
> *And put an end to his cursed government.*
> *But as you are weak and poor in spirit*
> *and in power and in authority,*
> *Down with you for all eternity. Amen.*[107]

The ultimate aim of Communism in conquering new countries is not to establish another social or economic system. It is to mock God and praise Satan.

The German Socialist Student Union has also published a parody of the Lord's Prayer, indicating that the 'true' meaning of the prayer upholds capitalism:

*Our Capital, which art in the West,*
*May your investments be sure,*
*May you make a profit*
*May your shares increase in value,*
*On Wall Street as in Europe,*
*Our daily sale give us today, and extend our credits,*
*As we extend those of our debtors.*
*And do not lead us into bankruptcy,*
*But deliver us from the trade unions,*

*For thine is half the world and the power,*
  *and the riches, for 200 years.*
                                    *Mammon.*[108]

The identification of Christianity with the interests of capitalism is outrageous. The church knows that capitalism, too, is stained with blood. Every economic system bears the marks of sin. Christians oppose Communism not from the viewpoint of capitalism but of the Kingdom of God, which is their social ideal. The above is nothing less than satanic mockery of the most holy prayer, just like the one published by the Soviets.

Mockery of the Lord's Prayer is customary in many Communist lands. Ethiopian children are taught to pray as follows:

*Our Party which rulest in the Soviet Union,*
*Hallowed be thy name,*
*Thy Kingdom come,*
*Thy will be done in Ethiopia*
*and in the whole world.*
*Give us this day our daily bread,*
*and don't forgive the trespasses*
*of the Imperialists as we will not*
*forgive them.*

> *And may we resist the temptation*
> *to abandon the fight,*
> *And deliver us from the evils of*
> *Capitalism. Amen.*

Over the Lutheran radio station confiscated by the Communist government a Satanist version of the Bible is broadcast. 1 Corinthians 13 sounds like this:

'Though I speak all the languages and have no enmity towards the landlords and capitalists, I have become as sounding brass . . . Class hatred suffers no exploitation and is brutal. Class hatred envies their riches and vaunts itself with the successful revolutions in many Socialist states . . . And now abide faith, hope, and class hatred, but the greatest of these is revolutionist hatred.'

During the general strike organised by the French Communists in 1974, workers were called to march in the streets of Paris shouting the slogan,

> *'Giscard d'Estaing est foutu,*
> *Les démons sont dans la rue!'*

(Giscard de'Estaing [the French president] is done with. Demons are now in the street.) Why 'demons'? Why not 'the proletariat' or 'the people'? Why this evocation of satanic forces? What has this to do with the legitimate demands of the working class to have better salaries?

## Deification of Communist Leaders

Communist leaders have been and are deified. Listen to the following poem honouring Stalin in *Pravda* (Moscow, 10 March, 1939; *Pravda* is the central organ of the Communist Party in the U.S.S.R.):

*The sun shines mildly and who would not know that you*
*    are this sun?*
*The pleasant noise of the sea waves sings an ode to Stalin.*
*The blinding snowy peaks of mountains sing the praise of*
*    Stalin.*
*The millions of flowers and meadows thank you.*
*Likewise the covered tables.*
*The beehives thank you.*
*The fathers of all young heroes thank you, Stalin;*
*Oh, Lenin's heir, you are for us Lenin himself.*

Thousands of such poems have been composed.
Here is another hymn to Stalin of extraordinary
fervour and beauty, reminding one of Eastern Byzantine Christianity in the fourth and following
centuries:

> *O great Stalin, O leader of the peoples,*
> *Thou who broughtest man to birth,*
> *Tho who purifiest the earth,*
> *Thou who restorest the centuries,*
> *Thou who makest bloom the Spring,*
> *Thou who makest vibrate the musical chords . . .*
>
> *Thou, splendour of my Spring, O Thou*
> *Sun reflected from millions of hearts.*

The foregoing hymn was published in *Pravda* in
August 1936. In May of 1935 the same official Party
newspaper had published the following extraordinary effusion:

*He commands the sun of the enemies to set.*
*He spoke, and the East for friends became a great glow.*
*Should he say that coal turns white.*
*It will be as Stalin wills . . .*
*The master of the entire world—remember—is now Stalin.*

A much later composition by a leading Soviet poet

shows development in style but hardly in subject matter:

*I would have compared him to a white mountain—but the mountain has a summit.*
*I would have compared him to the depths of the sea—but the sea has a bottom.*
*I would have compared him to the shining moon—but the moon shines at midnight, not at noon.*
*I would have compared him to the brilliant sun—but the sun radiates at noon, not at midnight.*

Mao-Tse-Tung has been hailed as the one 'whose mind created the world.' Kim-Il-Sung, dictator of North Korea, is also deified, as is Nicolaie Ceaushescu, Communist dictator of Romania.

Ceaushescu is another Satanist figure. He is the object of a personality cult and is likened to Julius Caesar, Alexander the Great, Pericles, Cromwell, Napoleon, Peter the Great, Abraham. This distinguished roster, it seems, is not enough. So he is also called *'Our lay God.'*

Communist Romania, which does not allow international religious conventions, permitted a witches' convention in the spring of 1979 in Curtea De Argesh.

In Bucharest there is a museum containing gifts brought by the people to Ceaushescu. In it is a water-colour painted by a blind man, who regained his sight through a miracle. He attributes it to the fact that 'he concentrated all his thoughts on the President, who not only can make the blind to see but can move the Carpathian mountains.'

Another portrayal shows Ceaushescu with King Vlad Tsepesh, who was known as 'the vampire Dracula' because he used to impale his adversaries. In similar fashion, Stalin magnified the personality of Czar Ivan the Terrible.[109]

62

# The Little and the Big Devils

According to official Marxist doctrine, which as has been illustrated, is only a disguise, neither God nor the devil exists. Both are fancies. Because of this teaching, Christians are persecuted by the Communists.

However, the Soviet newspaper *Kommunisma Uzvara* of April 1974 reports that many atheist circles have been created in Red Latvia's schools. The name given the children in those circles from 4th through 6th grade is 'Little Devils', while 7th graders are called 'Servants of the Devil.' In another school 8th graders have the name 'faithful Children of the Devil.' At the meeting the children come clothed as devils, with horns and tails.[110]

Thus, it is forbidden to worship God, but devil-worship is openly permitted and even encouraged among children of school age. This was the hidden objective of the Communists when they seized power in Russia.

In Vietebsk (U.S.S.R.), Zoia Titova, member of the Communist youth organisation, was caught practising black magic. When her case was brought before the assembly of Communist youth, there was unanimous refusal to punish her, though members who decide to worship God are expelled. The Communists consider it wrong to believe in God. For this 'crime', many children have been separated from their families and kept in special atheist boarding schools.

Moreover, the Communists wanted to make Satan-worshippers of church leaders. The Russian Orthodox priest Platonov, an anti-Jewish agitator, went over to the side of the Communists when they came to power in Russia. For this he was made a bishop and became a Judas who denounced members of his flock to the Secret Police, well knowing they would be persecuted. One day on a bus he met his sister Alexandra, an abbess who had been arrested many times, apparently with her brother's knowledge. He asked her, 'Why don't you speak to me? Don't you recognise your brother?' She answered, 'You ask why? Father and mother would turn over in their graves. You serve Satan.' Though an official Orthodox bishop in the Soviets, he replied, 'Perhaps I am Satan myself.'[111]

*Pravoslavnaia Rus* writes, 'The Orthodox cathedral in Odessa, so much loved by the Odessites, became the meeting-place of Satanists soon after the Communists came to power . . . They gathered also in Slobodka-Romano and in Count Tolstoi's former home.' Then follows a detailed account of Satanist masses said by deacon Serghei Mihailov, of the treacherous Living Church, an Orthodox branch established in connivance with the Communists. An attendant describes the Satanist mass as 'a parody of the Christian liturgy, in which human blood is used for communion.' These masses took place in the cathedral, before its main altar.

Also in Odessa, a statue of Satan used to be exhibited in the Museum of the Atheists. It was called Bafomet. At night, Satanists would gather in the museum for prayer and chanting before the statue.[112]


## Religious Obscenities

It might be understood that Communists would arrest priests and pastors as counter revolutionaries. But why were priests compelled by the Marxists in the Romanian prison of Piteshti to say the mass over excrement and urine? Why were Christians tortured to take communion with these as the elements? Why the obscene mockery of religion? Why did the Romanian Orthodox priest Roman Braga, whom I knew personally when he was a prisoner of the Communists, and who presently resides in the

U.S.A., have his teeth knocked out one by one with an iron rod to make him blaspheme? The Communists had explained to him and others: 'If we kill you Christians, you go to heaven. But we don't want you to be crowned martyrs. You should curse God first and then go to hell.'

In the prison of Piteshti the Communists would force a very religious prisoner to be 'baptised' daily by putting his head into the barrel in which his fellow-sufferers fulfilled their necessities, meanwhile obliging the other prisoners to sing the baptismal service.

A theology student was forced to dress in white sheets (to imitate Christ's robe), and a phallus made out of soap was hung around his neck with a string. Christians were beaten to insanity to make them kneel before such a mocking image of Christ. After they had kissed the soap, they had to recite part of the liturgy.[113]

Prisoners were compelled to take off their trousers and sit with their naked bottoms on open Bibles.[114]

Such blasphemous practices were perpetrated for at least two years with the full knowledge of the Party's top leadership.

What have these indignities to do with Socialism and the well-being of the proletariat? Are their anti-capitalist slogans not merely pretexts for organising Satanic blasphemies and orgies?

Marxists are supposed to be atheists who believe in neither heaven nor hell. In these extreme circumstances Marxism has lifted its atheistic mask to reveal its true face, which is Satanism. Communist persecution of religion might have a human explanation; the fury of this persecution beyond any reason can only be Satanic.

In Romanian prisons and in the Soviet Union, nuns who would not deny their faith were raped anally and Baptist girls had oral sex enforced on them.[115]

Many died as martyrs. But the Communists were

not satisfied with this. Through Luciferian techniques they made martyrs die blaspheming in the delirium provoked by paroxysms of torture.

Only once in all his works did Marx ever write about torture. During his own lifetime, many of his followers were tortured by Russian Czarist authorities. Since Marx is usually described as a humanist, one would expect him to write with horror about this abominable practice.

But his only comment was, 'Torture alone has given rise to the most ingenious mechanical inventions and employed many honourable craftsmen in the production of the instruments.'[116]

Torture is productive, it produces inventions—this is all Marx had to say about the subject. No wonder Marxist governments have surpassed all others in torturing their opponents!

In 1923, there were in the Soviet Union mock trials of God, in the presence of Trotsky and Lunatcharski.[117] But such events do not belong only to the past.

Satanist desecrations of Catholic churches have occurred in the 1970s in Upyna, Dotnuva, Zanaiciu, Kalvarija, Sede, etc., localities in Soviet Lithuania. The most recent about which we know happened in Alsedeai on 22 September 1980.[118]

In his book *Psychiatric Hospital 14, Moscow*, Georgi Fedotov tells of his conversation with the psychiatrist Dr. Vladimir Levitski about the Christian Argentov detained there. The physician says, 'You are pulling your friend Eduard toward God and we toward the devil. So I'm using my rights as a psychiatrist to deny you and your friends access to him.'

The Christian Salu Daka Ndebele was interrogated by the Secret Police of Maputo, Communist Mozambique. The officer said to him, 'We want to kill your God.' He raised his gun toward the head of the prisoner and declared, 'This is my God. With this I have the power of life and death. If your God comes here, I will shoot Him dead myself.'[119]

In Chiasso, Communist Angola, Communists slaughtered animals in the church and placed their heads on the altar and pulpit. A poster proclaimed, 'These are the gods whom you adore.' Pastor Aurelio Chicanha Saunge was killed, together with 150 parishioners.[120]

When the Catholic Lithuanian priest Eugene Vosikevic was killed, the Communists evidently performed a Satanist ritual, because his mouth was found to have been filled with bread.[121]

*Vetchernaia Moskva*, a Communist newspaper, let pass a Freudian slip of the pen: 'We do not fight against believers and not even against clergymen. We fight against God to snatch believers from Him.'[122]

'The fight against God to snatch His believers' is the only logical explanation for the Communist fight against religion.

We do not wonder at these words in the Soviet newspaper.

Marx had said it already in his book *German Ideology*. Calling God 'the Absolute Spirit,' as his teacher Hegel had done, he wrote, 'We are concerned with a highly interesting question: the decomposition of the Absolute Spirit.'

It was not a fight against false belief in a nonexistent God that preoccupied him. He believed that God does exist and wanted to see this Absolute Spirit decompose, like many prisoners of the Communists who were made to rot in jail.

In Albania, the priest Stephen Kurti was sentenced to death for having baptised one child. Baptisms must be performed in secret in Albania and North Korea.

The prosecutor at the trial of Metropolitan Benjamin of Leningrad said, 'The whole Orthodox church is a subversive organisation. Properly speaking, the entire church ought to be in prison.'

The only reason all Christians are not in jail in the Soviet Union is that the Communists are not quite powerful enough. But the will to destroy everything is there. Unrestrained by the Spirit of God and empowered by the forces of evil, they would destroy the whole earth, including themselves.

In the Soviet Union baptisms can be officiated only after registration. Persons wishing to be baptised or have their child baptised must present their identity cards to the representative of the church board, who in turn must report them to the State authorities. The result is persecution. Kolkhozniks (workers on collective farms) have no identity cards and can therefore baptise their children only secretly.[123] Many Protestant pastors have received prison sentences for baptising people.

The Communist fight against baptism presupposes belief in its value for a soul. Religious people in Israel or Pakistan or Nepal oppose baptism in the name of their own religious outlook, because it is a Christian seal. But for atheists—as Communists declare themselves to be—baptism should mean just nothing. Supposedly it neither benefits nor harms the baptised. Why then do these Communists fight against baptism? It is because Communists 'fight against God to snatch believers from Him.' Their ideology is not really inspired by atheism.

'Among other purposes', said Lenin, 'we created our party specifically for the fight against any religious deceiving of the people.'

More about the relationship between Marxism and the occult can be found in *Psychic Discoveries Behind the Iron Curtain*,[124] by Sheila Ostrander and Lynn Schröder. It is highly significant that the Communist East is much more advanced than the West in research about the dark forces manipulated by Satan.

Dr Eduard Naumov, member of the International Association of Parapsychologists, was arrested in Moscow. The Moscow physicist L. Regelsohn, a

Hebrew-Christian who took his defence, tells us the reason for his arrest: Naumov endeavoured to keep the psychic sphere of life free from the domination of evil forces that used parapsychology as a new weapon only for the oppression of the human soul.[125]

In Czechoslovakia, Bulgaria, etc., the Communist Party spends huge sums on secret investigation into this science. There is an Iron Curtain which does not allow the West to know anything about what happens in the twenty parapsychological institutes located in the Soviet Union.

*Komsomolskaia Pravda* (Moscow) published a lengthy article about hypnotists who make people 'regress to past lives.'

For the induction process they use the following suggestions: 'You descend into earth, deeper, even deeper. You and the earth become one . . . You are deep in the earth. You are surrounded by thick darkness . . . Around you is eternal night . . .

'Now we approach a spot of light far away . . . nearer and nearer. We sneak through a small hole to the sky, leaving our own body deep in the earth . . . We overcome the frontiers of time . . . and we return to your past . . .'

In such articles the Soviets use intentional double talk. Aware that some might become frightened, they are purposefully reserved, claiming they only inform without agreeing.

But what would readers think of an editor who reprinted provocative articles and lustful pictures endlessly from *Playboy* while claiming that he did not agree fully with what he was purveying to the public?

Soviet writers say clearly that this 'time machine' is not science fiction. 'Transpersonalism' offers this voyage in time.

In the Satanist black masses, all prayers are said from the end to the beginning, and the priestly robe is worn inside out. Inversion is the Satanist rule, which is applied even to the doctrine of reincar-

69

nation. Whereas Indian devotees are concerned about their future reincarnations and try to better themselves by obeying what they believe to be God's commandments, the Satanists offer a return to former incarnations. They care nothing about a better future in eternity.

## Marxism as a Church

Just as Satan came to Jesus with Bible verses, so Marx used texts of Scripture, with much distortion.

Volume 2 of the *Works of Marx and Engels* opens with Jesus' words to His disciples (John 6:63), as quoted by Marx in his book *The Holy Family:* 'It is the spirit which gives life.' Then we read: 'Criticism [his criticism of all that exists] so loved the masses that it sent its only-begotten son [i.e., Marx], that whoso-ever believes in him should not perish but have a life of criticism. Criticism became masses and lived among us, and we saw its glory as the glory of the only-begotten Son of the Father. Criticism did not consider it robbery to be equal with God, but made itself of no reputation, taking the form of a book-binder, and humbled itself up to nonsense yes, critical nonsense in foreign languages.'[126]

Those knowledgeable in Scripture will recognise this as a parody of Biblical verses. (John 3.16; 1:14; Philippians 2.6–8) Here again, Marx declares his own works to be 'nonsense', as well as 'swinish books.'

Marxism is a new religion. It uses Scripture. Its main work, *The Capital* by Marx, is called 'the Bible of the working class.' Marx considered himself 'the Pope of Communism.'[127]

Communism 'has the pride of infallibility.'[128] All who oppose the Communist 'creed' (this expression is used by Engels[129]) are excommunicated. Marx wrote, 'Bakunin should beware. Otherwise we will excommunicate him.'[130]

Those who died in the service of Marxism are feasted as 'martyrs.' Marxism has its sacraments: the solemn receptions in the toddlers' organisation 'the Children of October', the oaths given when received as 'Pioneers', after which come the higher grades of initiation in the Komsomol and the Party. Confession is replaced with public self-criticism before the assembly of Party members.

Marxism is a church. It has all the characteristics of a church. But its god is not named in its popular literature. In this book I have provided the proof that Satan is its god.

It is strange that, though Marxism is clearly satanic, it is not seen as a threat by many churches in the free world. Some illuminating statistics are available.

Seminary professors in the U.S.A. were asked, 'Can an individual consistently be a good member of your denomination and adhere to Marxism?'

Below are the percentage figures of those who answered Yes:[131]

|  | % |
| --- | --- |
| Episcopalian | 68 |
| Lutheran | 53 |
| Presbyterian | 49 |
| Methodist | 49 |
| Church of Christ | 47 |
| American Baptist | 44 |
| Roman Catholic | 31 |

## Marx and Darwin

What was the specific contribution of Marx to Satan's plan for mankind? It was important.

The Bible teaches that God created man in his own image (Genesis 8:24) Up to the time of Marx, man continued to be considered as the 'crown of creation.' Marx was Satan's chosen tool to make man lose his self-esteem, his conviction that he comes from high places and is meant to return to them. Marxism is the first systematic and detailed philosophy which reduces abruptly the notion of man. According to Marx, man is primarily a belly which has to be constantly filled and refilled. The prevailing interests of man are economic in nature. He produces in order to satisfy his needs. For this purpose he enters into social relationships with other men. This is the basis of society, what Marx calls 'infrastructure.' Marriage, love, art, science, religion, philosophy, everything other than the needs of the belly, are all 'superstructure', determined in the last analysis by the state of the belly.

No wonder Marx rejoiced greatly upon reading Darwin's book *The Descent of Man*, another masterstroke to make men forget their divine origin and divine purpose. Darwin said that man springs from the animal world and has no aim other than mere survival.

Man, who was given dominion over nature, was dethroned by these two. Satan could not dethrone God, so he devalued man. Man was shown to be the progeny of animals and a servant to his intestines.

It is a coincidence that the 19th century gave the world three leading personalities opposed to Christianity, all bearing the name of Charles:

Karl (German for Charles) Marx, Charles Darwin, and the French poet Charles Baudelaire. The latter wrote in *Abel and Cain:*

> *Race of Cain, ascend to heaven*
> *And throw God to the earth.*

Marx wrote to Ferdinand Lassalle on 16 January 1861, 'Darwin's book is very important and serves me as a basis in the natural sciences for the historical class struggle.'

Marx's son-in-law, Paul Lafargue, in *Socialism and*

*the Intellectuals* says, 'When Darwin published his *Origin of Species*, he took away from God his role as creator in the organic world, as Franklin has despoiled him of his thunderbolt.' The terrible thing is that it was not Darwin's original intent to harm religion. He had written, 'There is a grandeur in this view of life, with its several powers, having been originally breathed into a few forms or into one.' In order to make his position more emphatic, Darwin inserted the phrase 'by the Creator' after 'breathed' in the second edition. It remained there in all the succeeding editions he published.

Later, Freud would complete the work of these two satanic giants, reducing man basically to a sex-urge, sublimated sometimes in politics, art or religion. It was the Swiss psychologist Carl Gustav Jung who returned to the Biblical doctrine that the religious impulse is man's basic urge.

The age of Marx was a time of Satanist ferment in many spheres of life. It was the period in which the French poet Baudelaire wrote *The Flowers of Evil*, proclaiming himself openly to be on the side of immorality. The Russian poet Sologub, wrote, 'My father is the devil'; another Russian poet, Briusov, 'I glorify equally the Lord and the devil.'

Marx was a child of the time that also gave us Nietzche (Hitler's and Mussolini's favourite philosopher), Max Stirner, an extreme anarchist, and Oscar Wilde, the first theoretician of freedom for homosexuality, a vice which today has met with acceptance even among the clergy.

Satanic forces prepared Russia for the victory of Marxism. The time of the revolution was a period when love, good will, and healthy feeling were considered mean and retrograde. Girls hid their innocence and husbands their faithfulness. Destruction was praised as good taste, neurasthenia as the sign of a fine mind. This was the theme of new writers who burst on the scene out of obscurity. Men invented vices and perversions, and were fastidious in their avoidance of being thought moral.

How was it that Stalin became a revolutionist after reading Darwin?[132] As a student in the Orthodox seminary he obtained from Darwin the concept that we are not creatures of God but the result of an evolution in which ruthless competition reigns. It is only the strongest and most cruel who survive. He learned that moral and religious criteria play no role in nature and that man is as much a part of nature as a fish or an ape. Then long live ruthlessness and cruelty!

Darwin had written a scientific book setting forth his theory of origins. It had no economic or political implications. But though many might go so far as to concede that God created the world through a long process of evolution, the end result of Darwin's theory has been the killing of tens of millions of innocents. He therefore became the spiritual father of the greatest mass-murderer in history.

Beyond the intellectual turmoil of the nineteenth century can be traced the influence of the French Revolution, which was spiritually very much akin to the Russian cataclysm of the twentieth century.

During the upheaval in France, Anarchasis Clootz, a leading French revolutionary and Illuminatus, declared himself to be 'the personal enemy of Jesus Christ.' He proclaimed before the Convention on 17 November 1792, 'The people is the Sovereign and the God of the world . . . Only fools believe in any other God, in a Supreme Being.' The Convention then issued a decree proclaiming 'the nullification of all religions.'

All these aspects need to be studied. I call upon scholars to do so.

For those of us who take seriously the words of the Lord's Prayer, 'Deliver us from evil', the meaning is clear: we implore a loving God to protect us and society around us from false doctrine, from pernicious art that accustoms us to evil under the guise of beauty, and from immorality in life. Then we need have no fear of the devil's snares.

You have the choice: do you want to become like a devil, cruel and vicious, or like Jesus, the God-man of holy love and peaceful soul?


## Moses Hess's False Zionism

To complete the picture, we adduce a few more words about Moses Hess, the man who converted Marx and Engels to the Socialist ideal.

There is a tombstone in Israel inscribed with the words, 'Moses Hess, founder of the German Social-Democrat Party.' Hess expounds his beliefs in the *Red Catechism for the German People:* 'What is black? Black is the clergy. . . . These theologians are the worst aristocrats . . . The clergyman teaches the princes to oppress the people in the name of God. Secondly, he teaches the people to allow themselves to be oppressed and exploited in God's name. Thirdly and principally, he provides for himself with God's help a splendid life on earth, while the people are advised to wait for heaven . . .'

'The Red flag symbolises the permanent revolution until the completed victory of the working classes in all civilised countries: the Red republic . . . The Socialist revolution is my religion . . . The workers, when they have conquered one country, must help their brethren in the rest of the world.'[133]

This was Hess's religion when he first issued the *Catechism.* In the second edition, he added a few chapters. This time the same religion, i.e., the Socialist revolution, uses Christian language in order to accredit itself with believers. Together with the propaganda of revolution, there are indeed a few nice words about Christianity as a religion of love and humanity. But its message must be made clearer:

its hell must not be on earth and its heaven beyond. The Socialist society will be the true fulfilment of Christianity. Thus Satan disguises himself as an angel of light.

After Hess convinced Marx and Engels of the Socialist idea, claiming from the very beginning that its purpose would be to give 'the last kick to medieval religion'.[134] His friend Georg Jung said it even more clearly: 'Marx will surely chase God from his heaven'.[135] An interesting development took place in Hess's life: he who had founded modern Socialism also founded an entirely different movement, a specific brand of Zionism.

Thus Hess, founder of a socialism whose aim was to 'chase God from heaven', was also the founder of a diabolic type of Zionism that was to destroy godly Zionism, the Zionism of love, understanding and concord with the surrounding nations.

He who taught Marx the importance of class struggle wrote in 1862 these surprising words: 'Race struggle is primary, class struggle is secondary.'[136] He had lighted the fire of class war, a fire never extinguished, instead of teaching people to cooperate for the common good.

The same Hess then breeds a distorted Zionism, a Zionism of race struggle, imposed upon men who are not of the Jewish race. As we reject Satanic Marxism, so also must every responsible Jew or Christian reject this diabolical perversion of Zionism.

Hess claims Jerusalem for the Jews, but without Jesus, the King of the Jews. What need has Hess of Jesus? He writes, 'Every Jew has the making of a Messiah in himself, every Jewess that of a Mater Dolorosa in herself.'[137] Then why in the world did he not make of the Jew Marx a Messiah, a God-anointed man, instead of a hater bent on chasing God from heaven? For Hess, Jesus is 'a Jew, whom the heathen deified as their Saviour.'[138] Neither Hess nor the Jews seem to need Him for themselves.

Hess does not wish to be saved himself, and for an individual to seek personal sanctification is 'Indo-German', he says. The aim of the Jews, according to him, must be 'A Messianic state', 'to prepare mankind for the revelation of the divine essence',[139] which means, as he acknowledges in his Red Catechism, to make the Socialist revolution through racial and class struggle.

Moses Hess, who allotted to his idol Marx the task of putting an end to medieval religion, replacing it with the religion of Socialist revolution, writes these amazing words, 'I have always been edified by Hebrew prayers.'[140] What prayers do those who consider religion the opiate of the people say? We have seen already that the founder of scientific atheism prayed while wearing philacteries before burning candles. Jewish prayers can be misused in a blasphemous sense just as Christian prayers are in the Satanist ritual.

Hess had taught Marx that Socialism was insepar-able from internationalism. Marx writes in his *Communist Manifesto* that the proletariat has no father-land. In his *Red Catechism* Hess mocks the fatherland notion of the Germans. He would have done the same with the fatherland notion of any other Euro-pean nation. Hess criticised the Erfurt programme of the German Social-Democrat Party for its uncon-ditional recognition of the national principle. But Hess is an internationalist apart. Jewish patriotism must remain. He writes, 'Whoever denies Jewish nationalism is not only an apostate, a renegade in the religious sense, but a traitor to his people and to his family. Should it prove true that the emancipation of the Jews is incompatible with Jewish nationalism, then the Jew must sacrifice emancipation . . . The Jew must be, above all, a Jewish patriot.'[141]

I agree with Hess's patriotic ideas to the extent that what is sauce for the goose is sauce for the gander too. I am for every kind of patriotism—that of the

Jews, the Arabs, the Germans, the French, the Americans. Patriotism is a virtue if it means the endeavour to promote economically, politically, spiritually, and religiously the welfare of one's own nation, provided that it is done in friendship and cooperation with other nations. But the Jewish patriotism of a revolutionary Socialist who denies the patriotism of all other nations is highly suspect. This seems to me like a diabolic plan to make all peoples hate the Jews. If I were a non-Jew who saw the Jews accept Hess's plan of a unilateral patriotism, I would oppose it too. Fortunately, no Jews have accepted this satanic plan. In fact, it was Herzl who gave a sane turn to Zionism. In its modern form no trace of Satanism has remained.

The race struggle proposed by Hess is false, as false as the class struggle he enjoined.

Hess did not abandon Socialism for this specific kind of Zionism. After having written *Rome and Jerusalem*, he continued to be active in the world Socialist movement.

Hess does not state his thoughts clearly; therefore it is difficult to evaluate them. It is enough to know that according to him 'the Christian world views Jesus as a Jewish saint who became a pagan man.'[142] It is enough for us to read in his book, 'We today long for a far more comprehensive salvation than that which Christianity was ever able to offer.'[143] From *The Red Catechism* it follows that this more comprehensive salvation is the Socialist revolution.

It could be added that Hess was not only the original source of Marxism and the man who attempted to create an anti-God Zionism, but also the predecessor of the liberation theology current in the World Council of Churches, and of the new tendencies in Catholicism which speak about salvation. One and the same man, who is almost unknown, has been the mouthpiece of three Satanic movements:

Communism, a racist, hateful brand of Zionism, and liberation theology.

No one can be a Christian without loving the Jews. Jesus was Jewish, as were the virgin Mary and all the apostles. The Bible is Jewish. The Lord has said, 'Salvation is of the Jews' (John 4:22). Hess, on the other hand, exalts the Jews as though he consciously wanted to create a violent anti-Jewish reaction. He said that his religion was that of Socialist revolution. The clergy of all 'other' religions are crooks. Revolution is the only religion for which Hess has a high regard. He writes, 'Our religion (the Jewish) has at its point of departure the enthusiasm of a race which from its appearance on the stage of history has foreseen the final purposes of mankind and which had a foreboding of the messianic time in which the spirit of humanity will be fulfilled, not only in this or that individual or only partially but in the social institutions of all mankind.'[144] This time which Hess calls 'messianic' is the time of the victory of the Socialist world revolution.[145] The idea that the Jewish religion had as its point of departure the concept of a godless Socialist revolution is an ugly joke and an insult to the Jewish people.

Hess speaks persistently in religious terms, but he does not believe in God. He writes that 'our God is nothing more than the human race united in love.'[146] The way to arrive at such a union is the Socialist revolution, in which tens of millions of specimens of his beloved mankind will be tortured and killed. He makes no secret of the fact that he wishes neither the domination of heaven, nor that of earthly powers, which are both oppressive. There is no good in any religion, except that of social revolution. 'It is useless and inefficient to elevate the people to real freedom and to make them participate in the goods of existence, without freeing them from spiritual slavery, i.e., from religion.'[147] He speaks in one breath about 'the absolutism of celestial and earthly tyrants over slaves.'

The satanic depths of Communism can be understood only by knowing the kind of man Moses Hess was, for he influenced Marx and Engels, with whom he founded the First International, as well as Bakunin who joined them later.

Without a knowledge of Hess, Marx is unintelligible, because it is he who brought Marx to Socialism.

Let us remember Marx's words already quoted:

*Words I teach all mixed up into a devilish muddle.*
*Thus, anyone may think just what he chooses to think.*

Marx wrote in such a manner. Hess's writings are an even more devilish muddle, which is difficult to untangle but which has to be analysed for possible connections between Marx and Satanism.

Hess's first book was called *The Holy History of Mankind*. He proclaimed it to be 'a work of the holy spirit of truth',[148] saying further that as the Son of God freed men from their own slavery, Hess would free them also from political bondage. 'I am called to witness for the light, as John has been.'[149]

At that time, Marx, who was still opposed to Socialism and had not known Hess personally, started to write a book against him. For unknown reasons, this book was never completed. He became Hess's disciple later on.[150]

As previously indicated, Hess's avowed aims were to give the last kick to medieval religion and to produce ravages. In the introduction to his book *Last Judgment*, he declares his satisfaction that the German philosopher Kant had allegedly 'decapitated the old Father Jehovah together with the whole holy family.'[151] (Hess covers his own ideas with the name of the great philosopher. Kant had had no such intentions. He had written to the contrary: 'I had to limit knowledge to make place for faith.')[152]

Hess declares the Jewish as well as the Christian religion to be 'dead',[153] which does not prevent him from writing in *Rome and Jerusalem* about 'our holy writings', 'the holy language of our fathers', 'our cult', 'the divine laws', 'the ways of Providence', and 'godly life.'[154]

It is not that at different stages in life he had held different opinions—in his pseudo-Zionist book he declares that he does not disown his former godless endeavours. No, this is an intentional 'devilish muddle.'[155]

Hess was Jewish and a forerunner of Zionism. Because Hess, Marx, and other people like them were Jewish some people consider Communism a Jewish plot. Yet Marx also wrote an anti-Jewish book. In this respect, too, he has simply followed Hess. This 'Zionist' who elevates Jewry to heaven wrote in his book *About the Monetary System:* 'The Jews, who had the role, in the natural history of the social animal world, to develop mankind into a savage animal, have fulfilled this, their professional job. The mystery of Judaism and Christianity has been revealed in the modern Judeo-Christian. The mystery of the blood of Christ, like the mystery of the old Jewish worship of the blood, appears here unveiled as being the mystery of the predatory animal.'[156]

Don't worry if you fail to understand these words. They were written 'mixed up into a devilish muddle', but the hatred for Jewishness contained in them is clear. Hess is a racist, Jewish as well as anti-Jewish, according to the needs of the spirit which inspired his works and which he calls 'holy.'

Hitler could have learned his racism from Hess. He who had taught Marx that social class is a decisive factor also wrote the contrary: 'Life is an immediate product of race.'[157] Social institutions and conceptions, as well as religions, are typical and original creations of the race. The problem of race lies hidden behind all the problems of nationalities and freedom.

All of past history was concerned with the struggle of races and classes. Race struggle is primary; class struggle is secondary.[158]

How will Hess manage to have so many contradictory ideas triumph? 'I will use the sword against all citizens who resist the endeavours of the proletariat.'[159] We will hear the same from Marx: 'Violence is the midwife which takes the new society out of the womb of the old one.'[160]

Marx's first teacher was the philosopher Hegel, who merely paved the way for Hess. Marx, too, had sucked poison from Hegel, for whom Christianity was wretched in comparison to the glorious past of Greek culture. He wrote: 'Christians have piled up such a heap of reasons for comfort in misfortune . . . that we ought to be sorry in the end that we cannot lose a father or a mother once a week', while for the Greek 'misfortune was misfortune, pain was pain.'[161]

Christianity had been satirised in Germany before Hegel. But he was the first to satirise Jesus Himself.

We are what we feed upon. Marx fed upon satanic ideas. Therefore he set forth Satanist doctrine.


## The Organisation 'Hell'

Communists have a habit of creating front organisations. All of the above suggests the probability that Communist movements are themselves front organisations for occult Satanism. This would explain why all the political, economic, cultural, and military weapons used against Communism have proved so inefficient. The means to fight Satanism are spiritual, not carnal; otherwise, while one Satanist front organisation, such as Nazism, is defeated, another will rise to greater victory.

Himmler, the minister of Interior Affairs of Nazi Germany, thought himself to be King Henry the Fowler's reincarnation. He believed that it was possible to harness occult powers to serve the Nazi army. Several Nazi leaders were involved in black magic.

What was mere supposition when I published the first edition of this present book is now a proven fact. The proof has been given by the Communists themselves.

The story begins with the Netchaiev case, which prompted Dostoievsky to write his renowned novel *The Demons.*

Netchaiev, called a 'splendid, young fanatic'[162] by Bakunin, Marx's collaborator in founding the First International, wrote *The Catechism of the Revolutionist* as the guide for the Russian organisation 'Popular Revenge.' It appeared around 1870.

The purpose of this organisation was formulated as follows: 'Our cause is terrible, complete, universal, and pitiless destruction . . . Let us unite with the savage, criminal world, these true and only revolutionists of Russia.'[163]

The first man the Netchaiev group killed was one of their founding comrades, Ivanov, who dared to criticise his leadership. No criticism was permitted.

Netchaiev's plan was to divide mankind into two unequal parts. 'One tenth gets personal liberty and unlimited rights over the other nine tenths. These must lose their personality and turn into a kind of herd.'[164]

'They will engage in spy work. Each member of society will spy on the others and will be obliged to denounce . . . All are slaves and are equal in slavery.'[165]

Netchaiev wrote in his *Catechism:* 'A revolutionist must infiltrate everywhere, in the upper and lower classes . . . in churches . . . in literature.'

His disciple Peter Verhovensky commented: 'We are already terribly powerful . . . Jurors who acquit criminals are completely ours. The district attorney who trembles in courts not to be considered liberal enough is ours. Administrators, men of letters, we are many, very many, and they don't know they belong to us.'[166]

On the basis of such a programme an organisation with an impressive name was formed: 'World Revolutionist League.' Its constitution was signed by Netchaiev and Bakunin, Marx's intimate collaborator.[167] In the beginning it consisted of only a handful of men.

The revolutionist duke Peter Dolgorukov wrote on 31 October 1862: 'In London I met Kelsiev (who belonged to the above organisation), a narrow-minded but good man, terribly fanatical, with the face of a soft man. Kelsiev told me softly, with a benevolent look: "If we have to slaughter, why not slaughter, provided this is useful?" . . . All these London men speak continually about "burning down, slaughtering, cutting in pieces." These words have never left their tongue since Bakunin came to England . . .'

In 1869, in Geneva, Netchaiev wrote a proclamation in which, referring to the man who shot the emperor Alexander II, he advises: 'We must consider what Karakazov did as prologue. Yes, this was a prologue. Let us see to it that the drama itself begins soon.'[168]

From another proclamation: 'Soon, soon the day comes when we will unfurl the great flag of the future, the Red flag, and we will attack with great noise the Imperial palace . . .'

'We will have one shout, "To the axes!" and then we will kill the party of the emperor. Do not pity . . . Kill in public places if these base rascals dare to enter them, kill in houses, kill in villages.'

'Remember, those who will not side with us will be against us. Whoever is against us is our enemy. And we must destroy enemies by all means.'[169]

In 1872, a revolutionary society was formed under the simple name 'The Organisation', which has a super-secret kernel chillingly called 'Hell.' Though it has pursued its goals for well over a century, its existence was unknown to the outside world.

Soviet historians dared write about the activities of 'Hell', mentioning this circle, which was the fore-runner of the Russian Communist Party, only as recently as 1965—93 years after its formation.

In *Revolutionist Underground in Russia*, E. S. Vilen-skaia wrote: ' "Hell" was the name of the centre above the secret organisation, which not only used terror against the monarchy, but also had punitive functions toward the members of the secret organisation.'[170]

In *Tchernishevsky or Netchaiev*,[171] we read that one of the members (Fediseev) of 'Hell' took it upon himself to poison his own father in order to give the organisation his inheritance.

Tchernishevsky, who belonged to this movement, wrote, 'I'll participate in revolution; I am not fright-ened by dirt, by drunkards with sticks, by slaughter. We don't care if we have to shed thrice as much blood as the rebels in the French revolution. So what if we had to kill a hundred thousand farmers?'

Here are some of the expressed aims of the satanic organisation: 'Mystification is the best, almost the only means to impel men to make a revolution.' 'It is enough to kill a few million people and the wheels of revolution will be oiled.' 'Our ideal is awful, complete, universal, and pitiless destruction.'

And finally: 'Mankind must be divided into two unequal parts. One-tenth receives personal liberty and unlimited rights over the other nine-tenths. The latter must lose their personality and become a kind of herd.'[172]

In their writings, we continually find the phrase 'we are not afraid'. A typical example is the following proclamation: 'We are not afraid that we might find out three times more blood will have to be shed for the overthrow of the existing order than the Jacobins (French revolutionists) had to shed in their revolution in 1790 . . . If for the fulfilment of our objectives we had to slaughter 100,000 landlords, we would not be afraid of this either.'[173]

In reality, the number of victims was much greater. Churchill says in his *Memoirs of World War II* that Stalin confessed that 10,000,000 people died as a result of the collectivisation of agriculture in the Soviet Union.

The important fact to remember is that the Communists have now confessed, after a delay of almost a hundred years, that at the inception of their movement was a circle called 'Hell.' Why 'Hell'? Why not 'The Society for the Betterment of the Poor' or '. . . of Mankind'? Why the stark emphasis on Hell?

Today the Communists are more cautious. But in the beginning their very name revealed that their avowed aim was to recruit men for eternal damnation.

## Orginform

A gigantic organism has been created by the Soviet Secret Police to destroy the churches in the whole world. Their first aim is to cancel or minimise the hostility of religions toward Communism. Additionally, they seek allies within the churches so they may use clerical prestige to bring the mass of believers into the camp of revolution. The name of this department is Orginform. It has secret cells in every country, in every large religious organisation. One can assume that anti-Communist organisations and missions working behind the Iron Curtain are its main target. Communist agents specialising in propaganda and provocation infiltrate churches and missions to prepare the ideological disarmament of the faithful.

Its first director, Vassilii Gorelov, was formerly an Orthodox priest, an apostle turned Judas. The headquarters are in Warsaw. The actual leader is Theodor Krasky.

Orginform has one school in Feodosia for training agents for Latin countries and one in Moscow for North America. The agents for Britain, Holland, Scandinavia, etc., are trained in Siguel (Latvia) and those for Moslem countries in Constantza (Romania).

These schools prepare false pastors, priests, imams, and rabbis; each must understand thoroughly their respective theology. Some of them entrench themselves in churches or missions by posing as refugees.

The Jesuit Tondi, an Italian Communist, after attending the Lenin School in Moscow, was instructed by the Communist Party to enter a religious order. He became afterwards a secretary to Pope Paul VI. His true role was discovered. Now he openly declares himself to be a Communist and has married a comrade. He is still active in religious matters for the Communist Party and claims to have been forgiven by the Pope.[174]

## The Satanist Mass

Dr. Lawrence Pazder in *Michelle Remembers*[175] gives us the exact words of a highly secret Satanist mass, obtained through regression analysis from a girl who had attended such some twenty years before.

In the mass Satan appears and says:

> *Out of dark and fire red*
> *Comes a man of living dead;*
> *I only walk the earth at night,*
> *I only burn out the light.*
> *I only go where everybody's afraid;*
> *I go and find the ones who've strayed.*
> *All the darkest forces they are mine . . .*
> *Turn a light, make it night.*

Satan is obviously personified by the high priest of the sect. Then Satan takes a Bible in his hand and says:

> No eyes can see what this book said.
> What's written in the book is dead.
>
> No eyes can see, not even a friend.
> The books are mine in the end.
> You can write all day, you can write all night,
> But writing won't bring light.
> I'll burn it out. I'll make it black.
> I'll burn your words from front to back.
> I'll burn each page, I'll eat each word
> And spit it out never to be heard.
> The fire will grow, their eyes will see.
> The book of words can't stand up to me.
> When they grow old, they'll know and tell
> The only power comes from Hell . . .
>
> Matthew, Mark, Luke and John
> Burn in the fire and then you're gone.
> Their words were lies, my children will see.
> In the fire their word dies.
> The only thing left burning true
> Is the light that shows me to you . . .
>
> I'll be back, you wait and see.
> I'll be back to take the world for me.
> Everything that's gone must return.
> I was thrown out, but I can burn . . .
>
> Turn, my children, turn around.
> Touch every piece of ground.
> Touch everyone you can,
> Make a beast of every man.

Then follows the chant of the congregation:

> It's time to change from black to red.
> It's time to change from alive to dead.
> Prince of darkness . . .
> Help us celebrate the feast
> Of the coming of the Beast.

Satan again:

> The Holy One, the One most high—
> Ha, not for long; pretty soon it will be I . . .
>
> All the countries you see, I put my traps,
> Waiting for the boot to collapse.
> Money and numbers and the power to hate,
> These are the things on which I relate.
> Numbers of people—so many, each one small,
> Then, with so much money, the small are tall.

Friedrich Nietzsche, in the fourth part of *Thus Spake Zarathustra* under 'Awakening', provides the text of another black mass he himself composed. Its spirit does not differ much from the one above.[176]

Tragically, it has come to light that black masses have infiltrated the lives of many Americans, especially children.[177]

> Satan, Satan, Satan. He is God; he is God; he is God.

These blasphemous words are hidden in the lyrics of rock records that children listen to by the hour, many without even an awareness of what they are being subjected to. The words are hidden in the lyrics through a 'backward masking' technique.

'When the record is played forward, the message is received by the listener's subconscious mind which, like a computer, stores it away. The conscious mind hears one thing—the subconscious another.'

A number of rock groups have used the technique. Led Zeppelin's best-selling record 'Stairway to

Heaven', which admittedly, makes little sense as written, contains the masked message, 'I will sing because I live with Satan.' Another song contains the words, 'I decide to smoke marijuana.' Subliminal persuasion is more powerful, and therefore more dangerous than conscious influence.

Public black masses are rare today, but Stefan Zweig in his biography of Fouché describes one held in Lyon during the French Revolution.

A revolutionary, Chalier, had been killed. The black mass was celebrated in his honour. On that day crucifixes were torn from all the altars and priestly robes were confiscated. A huge crowd of men carrying a bust of the revolutionary descended on the marketplace. Three pro-consuls were there to honour Chalier, 'the God-Saviour who died for the people.'

The crowd carried chalices, holy images, and utensils used in the mass. Behind them was an ass wearing a bishop's mitre on its head. A crucifix and a Bible had been tied to its tail.

In the end, the Gospel was thrown into the fire together with missals, prayerbooks and ikons. The ass was made to drink from a Communion chalice as a reward for its blasphemous services. The bust of Chalier was put on an altar in place of the smashed image of Christ.

Tens of former Catholic priests participated in such actions.

A medal was issued to commemorate this event. Secret black masses do not take this shape, but the spirit is basically the same.

The Russian magazine 'Tunii Kommunist', Moscow, December 1984 describes in detail a Satanist mass in which bread and wine, mixed with dung and tears taken from operating on the eyes of a living cock, are 'transubstantiated' into the alleged body and blood of Lucifer.

During this ceremony the words of the mass are

read from the end to the beginning, as is customary in Satanist rituals. Then a covenant is concluded between Satan and his worshippers. The points of the contract are: renunciation of Christian teaching; new baptism in the name of the devil, with a change of name; renunciation of godparents, with the substitution of other protectors; bringing some personal clothing as a gift to Satan; swearing loyalty to Satan, while standing in a magic circle; inscription of the new member's name in 'The Book of the Dead', as opposed to Christ's Book of Life; the promise to consecrate one's children to the devil, as well as gifts and deeds pleasing to him; an oath to keep the secrets of the witches' coven and to demean the Christian religion.

Why would Communists dig out such teachings from old books of demonology and recommend them to the youth, saying 'they are rich food for thought?' Is that in essence all that Marxism has to offer the human mind?

The Communist magazine continues: 'In this devilish anti-world, which externally is completely like ours, man must reply with evil to every success in life.' Then it brazenly affirms the following as the slogan of the Satanist doctrinaire: 'Satan is not the foe of man. He is Life, Love, Light.'

The article ends with a quotation from Uspenskii expressing the hope of the Communists: 'There are ideas which touch the most intimate corners of our lives. Once these are touched, the marks remain forever . . . They will poison life.'[178]

This insidious material is presented in a subtle manner as if to provide information, but its aim is to arouse the reader's morbid curiosity, with ravaging effects.

During the initiation ceremony for the third degree in the Satanist church, the initiate has to take the oath, 'I will always do *only what I will.*' In other words, there is no authority beyond the polluted self.

91

This is an open denial of God's commandment, 'Seek not after your own heart and your own eyes, after which you used to go a whoring' (Numbers 15:39).

Marxists appeal to the basest passions, stirring up envy towards the rich and violence towards everyone. 'It is the evil side which makes history', wrote Marx, and he played a major role in shaping history.

Revolutions do not cause love to triumph. Rather, killing becomes a mania. In the Russian and Chinese revolutions, after the Communists had murdered tens of millions of innocents, they could not stop murdering. They brutally killed one another.

## Is Everything Permitted?

The Satanist cult is very old, older than Christianity. The prophet Isaiah might have had it in view when he wrote, 'We have turned every one to his own way; and the Lord has laid on him (the Saviour) the iniquity of us all' (Isaiah 53:6).

True religious feeling is at the opposite pole. There were Hassidic rabbis who never said 'I', because they considered it a pronoun that belonged only to God.

By way of contrast, when a man or woman is initiated into the seventh degree of Satanism, he swears that his principle will be, 'Nothing is true, and everything is permitted.' When Marx filled out a quiz game for his daughter, he answered the question 'Which is your favourite principle?' with the words, 'Doubt everything.'[179]

Marx wrote in *The Communist Manifesto* that his aim was the abolition not only of all religions but also of all morals, which would make everything permissible.

It was with a sense of horror that I read the mystery of the seventh degree of Satanism inscribed on a poster at the University of Paris during the 1968 riots.

It had been simplified to the formula, 'It is forbidden to forbid', which is the natural consequence of 'Nothing is true, and everything is permissible.'

The youth obviously did not realise the stupidity of the formula. If it is forbidden to forbid, it must also be forbidden to forbid forbidding. If everything is permissible, forbidding is permissible, too. Young people think that permissiveness means liberty. Marxists know better. To them, the formula means that it is forbidden to forbid cruel dictatorships like those in Red China and the Soviet Union.

Dostoievsky had said it already: 'If there is no God, everything is permitted.' If there is no God, our instincts are free. The ultimate expression of this kind of liberty is hatred. Whoever is free in this sense considers loving kindness a weakness of the spirit.

Engels said, 'Generalised love of men is an absurdity' (Anit-Duhring) The anarchist thinker Max Stirner, author of *The I and Its Property* and one of Marx's friends, wrote, 'I am legitimately authorised to do everything I am capable of.'

Communism is collective demon-possession. Solzhenitsyn in *Gulag Archipelago* reveals some of its horrible results in the souls and lives of people.

## The Mythical Marx

Let me say again that I am conscious that the evidence I have given to date may be considered circumstantial. The problem will have to be studied more thoroughly by someone else. But what I have written is enough to show that what Marxists say about Karl Marx is a myth. He was not prompted by concern for the poverty of his fellow men, for which revolution was the only solution. He did not love the proletariat but called them 'nuts', 'stupid', 'asses', 'rascals', even obscenities. (Correspondence with Engels.) He did not love even his comrades in the fight for Communism. He called Freiligrath 'the swine',[180] Lassalle 'Jewish nigger',[181] Bakunin 'a theoretical zero.'[182]

A lieutenant Tchekhov, a fighter in the revolution of 1848 who spent nights drinking with Marx, commented that Marx's narcissism had devoured everything good that had been in him.

Marx certainly did not love mankind. Giuseppe Mazzini, who knew him well, wrote that he had 'a destructive spirit. His heart bursts with hatred rather than with love toward men.'[183]

Mazzini was himself a 'Carbonari.' This organisation founded in 1815 by Maghella, a Genoan Freemason, declared its 'final aim to be that of Voltaire and of the French Revolution—the complete annihilation of Catholicism and ultimately of Christianity.' It began as an Italian operation but subsequently developed a broader European orientation.

Though Mazzini was critical of Marx, he maintained his friendship with him. The Jewish Encyclopaedia says that Mazzini and Marx were entrusted with the task of preparing the address and the constitution of the First International. This means that they were birds of the same feather, though they sometimes pecked at each other.

I know of no testimonies from Marx's contemporaries that contradicted Mazzini's evaluation. Marx the loving man is a myth constructed only after his death.

In fact, his favourite bit of verse was this quotation from G. Werth: 'There is nothing more beautiful in the world than to bite one's enemies.' In his own words, he said outright, 'We are pitiless. We ask for no pity. When our turn comes, we will not shun terrorism.' These are hardly the sentiments of a lover.

Marx did not hate religion because it stood in the way of the happiness of mankind. On the contrary, he simply wanted to make mankind unhappy in this world and throughout eternity. He proclaimed this as his ideal. His avowed aim was the destruction of religion. Socialism, concern for the proletariat, humanism—these were only pretexts.

After Marx had read *The Origin of Species* by Charles Darwin, he wrote a letter to Lassalle in which he exults that God—in the natural sciences at least—had been given 'the death blow.'[184] What idea, then, pre-empted all others in Marx's mind? Was it the plight of the poor proletariat? If so, of what possible value was Darwin's theory? The only tenable conclusion is that Marx's chief aim was the destruction of religion.

The good of the workers was only a pretence. Where proletarians do not fight for Socialist ideals, Marxists will exploit racial differences or the so-called generation gap. The main thing is that religion must be destroyed.

Marx believed in hell, and his programme, the driving force in his life, was to send men to hell.


## Robin Goodfellow

The documents proving Marx's connection with a Satanist sect continue to accumulate. Marx wrote, 'In the signs that bewilder the middle class, the aristocracy, and the prophets of regression, we recognise our brave friend, Robin Goodfellow, the old mole that can work in the earth so fast—the revolution.'[185]

Scholars who have read this apparently never looked into the identity of this Robin Goodfellow, Marx's brave friend, the worker for revolution.

The 16th century evangelist William Tyndale uses Robin Goodfellow as a name for the devil.[186] Shakespeare in his *Midsummer Night's Dream* calls him 'the knavish spirit that misleads nightwanderers, laughing at their harm.'[187]

Thus, according to Marx, considered the father of Communism, a demon was the author of the Communist revolution and was his personal friend.

In Argentina, groups of Communist terrorists kidnapped industrialists, demanded ransom money, and obtained millions. This money was multiplied in capitalist banks by a certain Graiver, who convinced poor people as well to entrust him with their savings. With the profits he financed terrorists. Then he went bankrupt, ruining the poor. Former presidents of Argentina and leading newspapermen were his accomplices, among them a man who had taken the name of Satanovsky.

It is worth remembering here that Stalin started writing under the pseudonyms 'Son of the devil' and 'Son of the demon.'


## Lenin's Tomb

In his revelation to St John, Jesus said something very mysterious to the church in Pergamos (a city in Asia Minor): 'I know where thou dwellest, even where Satan's seat is' (Revelation 2:13). Pergamos must have been a centre of the Satanist cult in that period. Now the world-famous Baedecker tourist guidebooks for Berlin state that the Island Museum contained the Pergamos altar of Zeus until 1944. German archaeologists had excavated it, and it had been in the centre of the Nazi capital during Hitler's Satanist regime.

But the saga of the seat of Satan is not yet over. *Svenska Dagbladet* (Stockholm) for 27 January 1948, reveals that:

1) The Soviet Army after the conquest of Berlin, carried off the Pergamos altar from Germany to Moscow. This tremendous structure measures 127 feet long by 120 feet wide by 40 feet high.

Surprisingly, the altar has not been exhibited in any Soviet museum. For what purpose was it transported to Moscow? We have already indicated that men in the top echelons of the Soviet hierarchy practice Satanist rituals. Have they reserved the Pergamos altar for their private use? There are many unanswered questions. Suffice it to say that objects of such high archaeological value usually do not disappear but are the pride of museums.

2) The architect Stjusev, who built Lenin's mausoleum, used this altar of Satan as a model for the mausoleum in 1924.[188]

Thousands of Soviet citizens wait in line every day to visit this sanctuary of Satan in which Lenin's mummy lies in state. Religious leaders of the whole world pay their homage to the Soviets 'patron saint' in this monument erected to Satan. Not a day goes by without wreaths of flowers being brought here, whereas the Christian churches on the same Red Square in Moscow have long since been turned into museums.

Satan rules in the Soviet Union in a highly visible manner.

The Satanist temple at Pergamos was only one of many of its kind. Why did Jesus single it out? Probably not because of the minor role it played at that time. Rather, his words were prophetic. He spoke about Nazism and Communism by which this altar would be honoured.

Since this is the story of Lenin's tomb, it is worth noting with irony that on the grave of his father there stands a cross with the inscription 'The light of Christ illuminates all' and a multitude of Bible verses.


## Call for Action

All these things I write in an exploratory manner. Christian thinkers, like other scholars, often succumb to the temptation to prove some preconceived ideas. They do not necessarily present only the truth as far as they have ascertained it. Sometimes they are prone to stretch the truth or exaggerate their argumentation in order to prove their point.

I do not claim to have provided indisputable proof that Marx was a member of a sect of devil-worshippers, but I believe that there are sufficient leads to imply this strongly. There are certainly enough leads to suggest Satanic influence upon his life and teachings, while conceding that there are gaps in the chain of evidence that would lead to a definitive conclusion in this matter. I have provided the initial impulse. Let others continue this important inquiry into the relationship between Marxism and Satanism.

Meanwhile, how can the church defeat Marxism?

The secular anti-Communist world can use the weapons of economic sanctions, political pressure, military threats, and broad-based propaganda. The church should certainly support any actions that conscience can endorse in the battle against the enemies of God. But it also has a weapon of its own.

The Ukrainian Metropolitan of the Catholic church, Byzantine rite, Andrew Count Sheptytsky, requested that Rome order prayers of exorcism against the Communists, whose 'regime cannot be explained except by a massive possession of the devil.'

Jesus did not tell His disciples to complain about demons but to cast them out (Matthew 10:8). I believe this can be effectively accomplished. However, this book is not the right forum for entering into details about such prayer.

# 4: Readers' Reactions

The first editions of this book produced interesting responses. Many greeted it as a new discovery in the understanding of Marxism and gave me valuable hints as to where I could find new material.

On the other hand, a Dutch personality dedicated several columns of his theological magazine to minimising the importance of the discovery. 'Well', he says, 'Marx may have indulged in black magic, but this does not count for much. All men are sinners, all men have evil thoughts. Let us not be alarmed at this.'

It is true that all men are sinners, but not all are criminals. All men are sinners, but some are murderers and some are the righteous judges who pass judgment on them. The crimes of Communism are unequalled. What other political system has ever killed sixty million men in half a century as have the Soviets?[189] Another sixty million have been killed in Red China—some estimates run much higher. There are degress of sinfulness and criminality. The enormity of crime is a measure of the intensity of Satanic influence on the founder of modern Communism. The sins of Marxism, like those of Nazism, surpass the ordinary. They are satanic indeed.

I have also had letters from Satanists offering an apology for their religion. One of them writes:

'A defence of Satanism needs only the Bible for documentary evidence. Think of all the thousands of earthly people, created in God's own image, mind you, destroyed by fire and brimstone (Sodom and Gomorrah), a lethal miscellany of plagues, and, to top everything off, the drowning of the earth's population, except for Noah's family. All of these devastations brought about by a "merciful" God/Lord/ Jehovah. What could a merciless god have done?

'But in all the Bible there is no record of even one death being brought about by Satan! So, let's hear it for Satan.'

This Satanist has not studied the Bible well. Death came into the world through Satan's deceit, his luring Eve into sin. This Satanist has also drawn his conclusions too soon. God has not yet finished with His creation.

Initially, every painting is a senseless, often ugly mixture of lines and dots of many colours. It took da Vinci twenty years to make of these the beautiful Mona Lisa. God also creates in time. In time he shapes beings and destroys them to give them a new form. The seed which has neither beauty nor fragrance dies as seed in order to become a splendid, perfumed flower. Caterpillars have to die as such in order to become beautiful butterflies. Men are allowed by God to pass through the refining fires of suffering and death. The apotheosis of creation will be a new heaven and a new earth in which righteousness will triumph. Then those who have followed Satan will have to suffer an eternity of regrets.

Jesus endured flogging and crucifixion. But whoever wants to know God must look beyond the tomb to Jesus' resurrection and ascension. In contrast, the enemies of Jesus who plotted his death brought their people and their temple to destruction and lost their own souls.

Our critic wished to comprehend God through reason, which is not the right instrument for a creature. God cannot be comprehended but only apprehended by a believing heart.

A Jamaican asks if the America that exploits his country is not as satanic as Marx. It is not. Americans are sinners, as are all men. America has a small group of devil-worshippers. But the American nation as such does not worship the devil.

*Nauka I Religia*, the principal atheist magazine of Moscow, contains a long article written by two philosophers, Belov and Shilkin. They say that 'Wurmbrand's temperament might be envied by the greatest football-players. His shouting is savage. This fighter calls for a crusade against Socialism, which he calls an offspring of Satan. He was imprisoned in Romania for distributing religious literature instigating revolt against the government!'[190]

In this article two things are to be noted: First, that I am called a 'devilish pastor' for my book *Was Karl Marx a Satanist?*, though the authors cannot produce one single fact to refute the documentation supporting Marx's links with a Satanist sect. Second, the article congratulates Christian leaders, even anti-Communists, who have taken a stand against me. They might be adversaries of Communism, but as long as they oppose Wurmbrand, chief enemy of Communism, they are approved by Moscow.

One remarkable letter came from a Nigerian who had been a labour union leader for twenty years. My writings helped him to see that he had been led astray by Satan. He has become a Christian.


## To All of You Marxists . . .

Now I address myself to the rank-and-file Marxist:

You are not animated by the spirit that controlled Hess, Marx, Engels. You really love mankind; you respect it and are confident you are enrolled in an army fighting for universal good. It is not your desire to be a tool of some weird Satanist sect. For you this book might be useful.

Satanic Marxism has a materialistic philosophy that blinds its followers to spiritual realities. But there exists more than matter. There is a reality of the spirit, of truth, beauty and ideals.

There is also a world of evil spirits, whose head is

Satan. He fell from heaven through pride and drew down with him a host of angels. Then he seduced the progenitors of the race. Since the Fall his deceit has been perpetuated and increased through every conceivable device, until today we see God's beautiful creation ravaged by world wars, bloody revolutions and counter revolutions, dictatorships, exploitation, racism of many kinds, false religions, agnosticism and atheism, crimes and crooked dealings, infidelities in love and friendship, broken marriages, rebellious children.

Mankind has lost the vision of God. But what has taken the place of this vision? Is it something better?

Man must and will have some religion. It is his nature to worship. If he has not a God-fearing religion, he will have the religion of Satan and will persecute those who do not worship his 'god.'

Presumably only a very few top leaders of Communism have been and are Satanists consciously, but there is also an unconscious Satanism, just as some people are basically Christian without knowing that their religion is that of Christ. A man can be a Satanist unconsciously without being aware that such a religion exists. He is so if he hates the notion of God and the name of Christ, if he lives as though he were only matter, if he denies religious and moral principles.

Those who delve into the occult are in the same class.

In Frankfurt, West Germany, more people go on Sunday to spiritualist meetings, where the dead are called up, than to church services. There are known Satanist churches in Munich and Dusseldorf, for instance.[191] There are many such churches in France, Britain, the U.S.A., and other countries.

In Great Britain there are 35,000 practising witches. American universities and even high schools offer courses in witchcraft, astrology, voodoo, magic, and

ESP. In France 40,000 black masses are conducted annually.

Human beings may forsake God, but God has never forsaken his creatures. He sent into the world His only Son Jesus Christ to save the race of man. Incarnate love and compassion lived on earth in the life of a poor Jewish child, then of a humble carpenter, and eventually of a teacher of righteousness. Downtrodden man cannot save himself, any more than a drowning man can fetch himself out of the water. So Jesus, full of understanding for our inner conflicts, took upon himself all our sins, including the sins of Marx and his followers, and bore the punishment for what we have done. He expiated our guilt by dying on a cross on Golgotha, after suffering the most terrible humiliation and agonising pain.

We have his word that whoever puts his faith in him is forgiven and will live with him in eternal paradise.

Even notorious Marxists can be saved. It is worth noting that two Soviet Nobel prize winners, Pasternak and Solzhenitsyn, both former Communists, after describing the extremities of crime to which satanic Marxism leads, have confessed their faith in Christ. Svetlana Alliluyeva, the daughter of Stalin the worst of the Marxist mass-murderers, also became a Christian.

Let us remember that Marx's ideal was to descend into the abyss of hell himself and draw all mankind in after him. Let us not follow him on this vicious path, but rather follow Christ who leads us upward to peaks of light, wisdom and love, toward a heaven of unspeakable glory.

## The Great Gulf

It is manifestly impossible to compare Jesus with Marx. Jesus is not greater or better than Marx. He belongs to an entirely different realm altogether.

Marx was human and probably a worshipper of the Evil One. Jesus is God, who reduced himself to the level of mankind with the desire to save it.

Marx proposed a human paradise. When the Soviets tried to implement it, the result was an inferno.

Jesus' kingdom is not of this world. It is a kingdom of love, righteousness and truth. He calls to everyone, including Marxists and Satanists: 'Come unto me, all ye that labour and are heavy laden, and I will give you rest' (Matthew 11:28). Believe in him, and you will have life eternal in his heavenly paradise.

There is no possibility of agreement between Christiantiy and Marxism, just as there can be no agreement between God and the devil. Jesus came to destroy the works of the Evil One (I John 3:8). As Christians follow him, they strive to destroy Marxism while retaining love for the individual Marxist and trying to win him to Christ.

Some proclaim that they are Marxist Christians. They either deceive or are deceived. One cannot be a Marxist Christian any more than one can be a devil-worshipping Christian.

Over the years, the Satanist aims of Marxism have not changed one bit.

The Marxist philosopher Ernst Bloch writes in his book *Atheism in Christianity* that 'the seduction of the first human couple by the serpent opens the way of salvation for mankind. So man starts to become a god; it is the way of rebellion. Priestcraft and the possessors of goods repressed this truth. The original sin consists in the fact that man does not wish to be like God. Man must conquer the power. The theology of revolution wills it that man should conquer the power of God. The world must be changed in the image of man. There should be no heaven at all. The belief in a personal God is the fall into sin. This fall must be repaired.'

There is a gulf between Chrisianity and Communism that can be bridged only in one sense: Marxists must abandon their devil-inspired teacher, repent of their sins, and become followers of Christ.

To help them cross over this bridge was the main purpose of this present work.

Marxists are concerned with social and political problems. These will have to be solved outside the tenets of Marxism. For Marx, Socialism was only a pretence. His aim was the diabolical plan to ruin mankind for eternity. By way of contrast, Christ desires our eternal salvation.

In the fight between Chrisianity and Communism, believers 'wrestle not against flesh and blood, but against principalities, against powers, against the rulers of the darkness of this world, against spiritual wickedness in high places' (Ephesians 6:12).

We have to choose not only between abstract good and abstract evil, but between God and Satan. Marx believed in God and hated him. Even in his old age he worshipped Satan as indicated earlier.

The average Marxist and the sympathiser of Marxism should not follow Marx in this spiritual aberration. Let us reject the bourgeois Marx, bearer of darkness, and Engels, factory owner and therefore, according to Marxist dogma, an exploiter. Let us rather choose the Light of the world and mankind's prime Benefactor, Jesus the working man, the Carpenter.

That Marxist Satanism has ravaged the world is terrible. That it has penetrated high places in the church is unthinkable. Yet such is the case.

To give just one example: the late Pope John Paul I praised Giuseppe Carducci, an Italian university professor, as an example of a good youth teacher.[192] Who is the man recommended by no less than the Pope?

Carducci became famous through his 'Hymn to Satan', which begins: 'My ardent verse is for thee. I invoke you, Satan, king of the feast.' It ends: 'In holiness, incense and vows should ascend to thee, Satan. You have defeated Jehovah, the god of the priests.'[193]

It would have been wrong for me to remain silent about these matters.

In 1949, a Soviet general said to a Catholic priest, Werenfried van Straaten, 'We are Satan's elite, but you, are you God's elite?'

We have seen in this book to what length devil-worshippers are willing to go. May their dedication to evil be an incentive for us to behave like God's elect!

During the troubles in Poland in 1982, one could see mocking inscriptions on the walls: 'Marx said, Proletarians of the world, forgive me!' instead of the usual 'Proletarians of the world, unite!'

I shuddered when I read these words.

It is said about Engels that he repented before his death. There is no such record about Marx, which means that he consigned himself to hell. In 1983, many commemorated the centenary of his death. Might he have held this same commemoration in hell?

While writing this book, I have passed many a sleepless night, thinking of what Marx must endure viewing in hell the rivers of tears and blood that he has caused to flow.

Jesus told a story about a rich man in the eternal fire who expressed one ardent desire: his brethren should be warned not to end up in the same place of torment.

Does Marx also have the same desire—that his followers should be warned not to walk in his footsteps leading to perdition?

Are the Polish people right when they have Marx say ' . . . forgive me'? Does he indeed cry out from the fire—as I truly believe in my heart of hearts—'Send someone to my house, for I have many comrades, that he may testify to them, lest they also come to this place of torment' (Luke 16:27, 28).

The Soviet Communists did an enormous wrong to their cause by disowning Stalin, who had become a popular idol. One can only speculate why they permitted such a reversal of policy, since it was certainly not in their best interest to remove Stalin's corpse from the mausoleum. Likewise, the Chinese Communists harmed their own cause by disowning Mao and jailing his wife.

Perhaps in the hidden depths of their souls, Soviet and Chinese Communist leaders have felt what is now the burning desire of their former idols, who too late are remorseful about what they have done and taught.

As for me, I love every man, including Marxists and Satanists. If Marx and Engels and Moses Hess were alive today, my most ardent wish would be to bring them to Jesus Christ, who alone has the answer to man's ills and the remedy for his sins.

This is my wish for you, the reader. You have walked with me through the terrible pages of this book. Now I urge you to consider carefully your loyalties before it is too late. Abandon Satan and his evil cohorts. History proves he is never true to his own. Therefore, choose life and love, and hope, and heaven.

Marxists and proletarians of the world, unite around Jesus Christ!

# Appendix

## Marxist 'Christian' Theology

Ernesto Cardenal is a Catholic priest who is at once a self-avowed Communist and a member of the Communist government of Nicaragua. He is one of the most prominent exponents of so-called Liberation Theology, which exists within both Catholicism and Protestantism and seeks to blend Christianity with Communism.

Here are a few excerpts from his book *The Zero Hour:*

'A world of perfect Communism is the kingdom of God on earth. They are the same thing for me . . . Through the Gospel I have arrived at revolution; not through Karl Marx, but through Christ. The Gospel caused me to become a Marxist . . . I have the calling of a poet and prophet . . .'

'Castro told me that the qualities of a good revolutionist are also the qualities of a good priest . . . Let us not forget that the first Christians were the best Christians, i.e., revolutionary and subversive Christians . . .'

'Marxism is a fruit of Christianity; without Christianity, Marxism would be impossible; Marx would be unthinkable without the prophets of the Old Testament. Changing the system of production, we can create the new man of the Gospel . . .'

'The Mexican Jesuit Jose Miranda says in his book *Marx and the Bible* that the Ten Commandments are Marxist, even the first commandment, to love God. For him, to love Jehovah above all means to love justice. If the church ever asserted anything else, it was a monstrosity.'

'I believe that the Communists, too, belong to the

church. I believe the true church includes many who don't perceive themselves as Christians, even those who consider themselves atheists. Many of these belong more to the church than some who sit in the Roman Curia.'

'Since Constantine, the church has always gone to bed with the capital. If Christians and Marxists would read each other's writings, there would be no conflicts any more between Christians and Socialism . . . It seems to me that worker-priests and revolutionists—the most progressive part of the church—are inspired directly by the Holy Ghost.'

'For me the God of the Bible is also the God of Marxism-Leninism . . . The apostle John says, "No one has seen God." What the atheist Marxists say is very much akin to what Saint John says: "No one has seen God." '

Another writer quotes Cardenal as follows: 'I am above all a revolutionist and as such fight for a Socialist country which is in the course of passing through a dictatorship of the proletariat, in which surely it cannot show itself feeble toward the enemies of its fatherland, not even in moments when one comes to the point of having to execute men for this purpose.'[194]

It is self-evident that a man who thinks like this has no trouble praising the regime in Cuba as a model of liberty.

Liberation Theology is not an isolated phenomenon.

It is the by-product of a general tendency to synthesise Marxism and Christianity; it is also seen in various forms of compromise in politics, art, economics, and so on.

Two Jews, Bernstein and Schwartz, composed the musical *The Mass* for the inauguration of the John Kennedy Centre for the Performing Arts in Washington in 1971. In it, during the singing of the Kyrie

Eleison, the Gloria, and the Credo, a band of singers and dancers howl their doubts:

> God made us the boss;
> God gave us the cross.
> We turned it into a sword
> To spread the word of the Lord.
> We use his holy decrees
> To do whatever we please. Yeah . . .

> Give us peace that we don't keep on breaking.
> Give us something or we'll just start taking.
> We're fed up with your heavenly silence,
> And we only get action with violence.

The 'Christian' multimillionaires present at the concert cheered. Their wives, apparelled in slit skirts and decollete bodices, bejewelled and befurred, joined in the applause. The music is now standard repertoire.

I can understand men like the priest Cardenal. There is a ring of truth in the feeling he expresses of solidarity with the Communists, who appear to him as champions of the cause of the poor—always near to the heart of Christians.

In the Bible Job is called a righteous man. He describes to his dubious friends the programme of his life: 'I delivered the poor that cried, and the fatherless, and him that had none to help him . . . I was a father to the poor: and the cause which I knew not I searched out. And I broke the jaws of the wicked, and plucked the spoil out of his teeth' (Job 29:12, 16, 17). These words could be uttered by any revolutionist.

Job continues: 'Did not I weep for him that was in trouble? Was not my soul grieved for the poor?' (30:25). 'If I did despise the cause of my manservant or of my maidservant when they contended with me, what then shall I do when God rises up?' (31:13, 14). True believers have always reacted like this.

Cardenal's assertion that 'the church has always gone to bed with the state' is untrue.

The war of secession in the U.S.A. which led to the abolition of slavery was influenced by the book of a Christian lady, Harriet Beecher Stowe, author of *Uncle Tom's Cabin*. She said simply, 'The Lord wrote it.'

During a Communion service she had a vision of an old slave being beaten to death by a white ruffian. This became the story of Uncle Tom's flogging.

The book was a stick of dynamite driven into the foundations of slavery, which had to disappear.

Charles Spurgeon, the greatest Baptist preacher of the last century, was also an ardent fighter against slavery. He wrote, 'If slavery is not wrong, nothing is wrong.' Wilberforce, a Christian and a capitalist, caused slavery to be abolished in the British Empire long before America's Civil War. Lincoln, also a Christian, issued the Emancipation Proclamation that freed the slaves in his own country.

The Theology of Liberation, which ignores these facts, is widely urged in the Third World. Its theoreticians can call themselves Christian only because of the chaotic thinking prevalent in the church at this moment. According to the Catholic rules, these theologians should long since have been expelled from the church.

According to the decree of 28 July 1949, of the Holy Office, the following categories of Catholics are excommunicated:

Whosoever belongs to the Communist Party;
whosoever makes propaganda for it in any way;
whosoever votes for it and its candidates;
whosoever writes for the Communist press, reads
    and spreads it;

whosoever remains a member in a Communist
    organisation;
whosoever confesses the materialistic and anti-
    Christian teaching of atheist Communism;
whosoever defends and spreads it.
This punishment applies also to parties that make
    common cause with Communism.

The revolutionist theologians belong only formally to
the Catholic Church, but they have a great influence
among believers. In the Orthodox churches, too,
there exists a tendency to exploit, for the benefit
of Communism, the spiritual energies that religion
awakens and channels. This will be the purpose of
an ecumenical council (the eighth) for which the
Soviet and Romanian official Orthodox churches are
preparing.

Its principal aim will be to proclaim an earthly
paradise. Communism is this paradise, Capitalism its
foe. The church no longer waits for the coming of
Jesus in the clouds of heaven. The triumph of
Communism will be equated with his coming.

This concept explains why in Romania, Czechoslovakia, and other Communist countries the God-
hating Communist government pays the clergy.

It needs to be said that among both Catholics and
Orthodox, there also exist contrary tendencies: fortunately, there are bishops who fear absorption into
earthly pursuits and seek rather a deeper spiritual
life.

As for Protestants, in hearings before the U.S.A.
House Committee on Un-American Activities on 26
February 1966, Richard Arens, general counsel to the
Committee, declared:

'Thus far, in the leadership of the National Council
of Churches, we have found over 100 persons in
leadership capacity with either Communist-front
records or records of services in Communist causes.

113

The aggregate affiliations of the leadership is in the thousands.'

The World Council of Churches for years has subsidised Communist guerrillas in Africa.

The Catholic Gustavo Gutierrez wrote in *The Theology of Liberation*: 'The church must place itself squarely within the process of revolution.' The Lutheran theologian Dorothee Solle, founder of 'Christians for Socialism', wrote: 'We are at the beginning of a new chapter in Christian history. It will not be written without Karl Marx.'

These are the facts, open and uncontested, about what is happening in the church universal.

## Perfect Communism: Kingdom of God on Earth?

Cardenal says, 'Communism and the kingdom of God are the same thing for me.'

The word 'Communism' in itself is vague. It is taken to mean only an economic system in which everyone will work according to his abilities and will receive according to his needs. There will be no state, no division of the world into countries, and no social classes, because the means of production will belong to all mankind.

Suppose this could be attained: where is God in the picture? Why should this be equated with the kingdom of God? A society of unbelievers, even of men who hate and scorn God, could choose or be forced to live in such a state.

Scripture says that when the kingdom is the Lord's, 'All the ends of the world shall remember and turn unto the Lord: and all the kindreds of the nations shall worship before him' (Psalm 22:27).

The kingdom of God will not be a stateless society. The people of the saints of the Most High will have dominion over it (Daniel 7:27).

It is not a kingdom brought about by a political

114

party, but Jesus, the Son of Man, shall come into his kingdom (Matthew 16:28).

Obviously, there will be none of the evils that plague society now, such as war, famine, pestilence, pollution, social injustice, exploitation, racism, etc. The kingdom of God will be one of righteousness, peace, love, joy, and the right to possess one's own mansion and garden (John 14:2). Father Cardenal, who asserts that he is a prophet, must know what his Biblical predecessor Micah said: 'In the last days . . . they shall sit every man under his vine and under his fig tree.' (4:1, 4) The prophet Isaiah reinforces this idea definitively: 'They shall not build, and another inhabit; they shall not plant, and another eat (65:22). Thus, Scripture endorses the notion of private ownership.

What would perfect Communism look like in reality? Perfection as we humans experience it is the ultimate achievement of years of practice—in the field of sports, music, typing, or skills of any sort. A violinist perfects his performance of a Beethoven concerto by practising his violin. A baseball pitcher achieves success by throwing the ball and refining his technique in intensive effort. A flautist who practises his craft does not automatically become a football hero.

Perfect Communism, described as economic liberation, freedom, peace, and justice can be attained only through the practice of such policies in the society it hopes to benefit.

Communists have jailed, tortured, and terrorised hundreds of millions of men for almost seventy years. How could such practice result in a just, mild, and loving society?

Christian Communism is a utopian nightmare. The theology of revolution is a patent absurdity, a contradiction in terms.

'What fellowship has righteousness with unrighteousness? And what communion has light with darkness? And what concord has Christ with Belial? Or what part has he that believes with an infidel?' (II Corinthians 6:14, 15).

'You cannot serve God *and* mammon', said Jesus. Choose you this day whom you will serve.

For correspondence with the author, inquiries and gifts for the underground church, the addresses are:

Christian Mission to the
Communist World
POB 19
Bromley Kent, BR1 1DY
Britain

Jesus to the Communist
World
PB 2947
Torrance 90509 California
USA

*Jesus to the Communist World*
PB 598
Penrith NSW 2750
Australia

*Voice of the Martyrs*
POB 476
Agege-Lagos
Nigeria

*Jesus to the Communist World*
PB 38
St. Thomas
Ontario
Canada

*Love in Action*
POB 4532
11–31 Green Park
New Delhi
India

*Jesus to the Communist World*
POB 11–295
Ellerslie
Auckland 5
New Zealand

*Christian Mission to the
Communist World*
POB 1145
Krugersdorp 1740
South Africa

# Interpretation of Abbreviations

Marx, Karl und Friedrich Engels, *Historisch-kritisch Gesamtausgabe. Werke, Schriften, Briefe. (Complete Historical Critical Edition. Works, Writings, Letters)* on behalf of the Marx-Engels Institute, Moscow, published by David Rjazanov. (Frankfurt-am-Main: Marx-Engels Archiv, 1927) This is MEGA, indicating Section, Volume, Part, and page numbers.

Marx, Karl und Friedrich Engels. *Werke. (Works)* (Berlin: Dietz-Verlag, 1974) This is MEW. The Volume number is in Roman numerals, the page number in Arabic numerals.

Marx, Karl and Friedrich Engels. *Collected Works.* (New York: International Publishers, 1974). This is CW, with Volume and page numbers.

Payne, Robert. *Marx.* (New York: Simon & Schuster, 1968). Cited as Payne. Emphasis in the quotations is by the author.

# Bibliographical Notes

1.  Karl Marx und Friedrich Engels, *Zur Kritik der Hegelschen Rechtsphilosophie (Critique of the Hegelian Philosophy of Law.* Introduction), MEGA, I, i (1), 607–608.
2.  Rev. Paul Oestreicher, *Sermons from Great St. Mary's* (London: Fontana, 1968), pp. 278–280.
3.  Karl Marx, *Die Vereinigung der Gläubigen mit Christo (The Union of the Faithful with Christ),* MEW, Suppl. Vol. I, 600.
4.  Karl Marx, *Betrachtung eines Junglings bei der Wahl eines Berufes (Considerations of a Young Man on Choosing His Career),* MEW, Supp. Vol. I, 594. Also Payne, 34.
5.  Karl Marx, *Das Kapital (The Capital)* (New York: Cerf & Klopfer, The Modern Library, 1906), p. 91.
6.  Karl Marx, *Archiv für die Geschichte des Sozialismus und der Arbeiterbewegung (Archives for the History of*

*Socialism and the Workers' Movement*), MEGA, I, i (2), 182–183.

7. Karl Marx, 'Des Verzweiflenden Gebet' ('Invocation of One in Despair'), *ibid.*, p. 30.
8. *Ibid.*, pp. 30–31.
9. Quoted in *Deutsche Tagespost*, West Germany, December 31, 1982.
9a. Bakunin, *Works* (Berlin, 1924), vol. III, p. 306.
10. Karl Marx, 'Spielmann' ('The Player'), *ibid.*, pp. 57–58.
11. Karl Marx, *Oulanem*, Act 1, Scene 1, *ibid.*, p. 60.
12. Act 1, Scene 2, *ibid.*, p. 63.
13. Act 1, Scene 3, *ibid.*, p. 68.
14. Karl Marx, *Louis Bonapart (The 18th Brumaire)*, MEW VIII, 119.
14a. MEW, I, 344; I, 380; XXVII, 190; VI, 234.
14b. Quoted in B. Brecht, *Works*, in 8 volumes (Frankfurt, 1979), vol. I, p. 651.
15. Marx, *Oulanem*, *loc. cit.*
16. *Ibid.*
16a. MEW, XXX, 359.
16b. Paul Goma, *Piteshti*.
17. Karl Marx, Letter of 10 November 1837 to his father, *ibid.*, p. 218.
18. Heinrich Marx, Letter of 10 February 1838 to Karl Marx, *ibid.*, p. 229.
19. Heinrich Marx, Letter of 2 March 1837 to Karl Marx, *ibid.*, p. 203.
20. Karl Marx, 'Hegel', *ibid.*, pp. 41–42.
21. Quoted in *Deutsche Tagespost*, West Germany, 31 December 1982.
22. Karl Marx, 'Das bleiche Mädchen' ('The Pale Maiden'), *ibid.*, pp. 55–57.
23. Müllern-Schönhausen, *The Solution of the Riddle, Adolf Hitler*.
24. Karl Marx, *Ueber die Differenz der demokritischen und epikureischen Naturphilosophie*. Vorrede (*The Difference Between Democritus' and Epicurus' Philosophy of Nature. Foreword*), *ibid.*, p. 10.
25. Jenny von Westphalen, *Mohr und General, Erinnerungen an Marx und Engels* (*The Moor and the General,*

*Remembrances about Marx and Engels*) (Berlin: Dietz Verlag, 1964), pp. 273–274.

26. Payne, p. 317.
27. *Ibid.*
28. Karl Marx, *Die Rheinische Zeitung* (*Rhine Newspaper*) Der Kommunismus und die Augsburger Allgemeine Zeitung (Communism and the Augsburger Allgemeine Newspaper), MEGA, I, i (1), 263.
29. Moses Hess, Letter of 2 September 1841 to Berthold Auerbach, MEGA, I, i (2), 261.
30. Georg Jung, Letter of 18 October 1841 to Arnold Ruge, *ibid.*, pp. 261–262.
31. Karl Marx, *Zur Kritik der Hegelschen Rechtsphilosophie. Einleitung* (*Critique of the Hegelian Philosophy of Law. Introduction*), MEGA, I, i (1), 614.
31a. MEW, I, 372.
31b. MEW, I, 386.
32. Hans Enzensberger, *Gespräche mit Marx und Engels* (*Conversations with Marx and Engels*) (Frankfurt-am-Main: Insel Verlag, 1973), p. 17.
33. James Hastings, *Encyclopaedia of Religion and Ethics* (New York: Charles Scribner's Sons, 1921), XI, 756.
34. Mikhail Bakunin, *God and the State* (New York: Dover Publications, 1970), p. 112.
35. Roman Gul, *Dzerjinskii* (Paris: published by the author, 1936. In Russian), p. 81.
36. Enzensberger, *op. cit.*, p. 407.
37. Pierre-Joseph Proudhon, *Philosophie de la Misère* (*The Philosophy of Misery*) (Paris: Union Générale d'Editions, 1964), pp. 199–200.
38. *Ibid.*, pp. 200–201.
39. Paul Garus, *History of the Devil* (Bell Publishing Co.), p. 435.
39a. Heinrich Heine, *Works*, vol. I, p. LXIV.
40. Charles Boyer, *The Philosophy of Communism*. 10. The Political Atheism of Communism, by Igino Giordani (New York: Fordham University Press, 1952), p. 134.
41. Karl Marx, 'Spielmann', *loc. cit.*
42. Jerry Rubin, *Do It* (New York: Simon & Schuster, 1970), p. 249.
43. Karl Marx, 'Menschenstolz' ('Human Pride'), MEGA, I, i (2), 50.

44. Karl Marx, Letter of 10 November 1837 to his father, *ibid.*, p. 219.

45. Georg Jung, Letter of 18 October 1841 to Arnold Ruge, *ibid.*, pp. 261–262.

46. Arnold Künzli, *Karl Marx, Eine Psychographie* (*Karl Marx, A Psychogram*) (Zürich: Europa Verlag, 1966)

47. David Rjazanov, *Karl Marx: Man, Thinker and Revolutionist* (*Karl Marx als Denker, Mensch und Revolutionär*) (New York: International Publishers, 1927)

48. Rolv Heuer, *Genie und Reichtum* (*Genius and Riches*) (Vienna: Bertelsmann Sachbuchverlag, 1971), pp. 167–168.

49. Karl Marx, Letter of 27 February 1852 to Friedrich Engels, MEW, XXVIII, 30.

50. Friedrich Engels, Letter of 2 March 1852 to Karl Marx, *ibid.*, p. 33.

51. Karl Marx, Letter of 8 March 1855 to Friedrich Engels, *ibid.*, p. 438.

52. Karl Marx, Letter of 2 December 1863 to Friedrich Engels, MEW, XXX, 376.

53. Franz Mehring, *Karl Marx—Geschichte seines Lebens* (*Karl Marx—Story of His Life*) Berlin: Dietz Verlag, 1964), pp. 99–100.

54. *Ibid.*, p. 97.

55. *Ibid.*, p. 100.

56. Bruno Bauer, Letter of 6 December 1841 to Arnold Ruge, MEGA, I, 1 (2), 263.

57. A. Melskii, *Evangelist Nenavisit.* (*The Evangelist of Hate—Life of Karl Marx*) (Berlin: Za Pravdu Publishing House, 1933. In Russian), p. 48.

58. Friedrich Engels, *Dialektik der Natur.* Finleitung (*Dialectics of Nature* Introduction), MEW, XX, 312.

59. Friedrich Engels, Poem probably written beginning 1837. MEGA, I, ii, 465.

60. Friedrich Engels, Letter of July 1839 to the Graber brothers, *ibid.*, p. 531.

61. Friedrich Engels, *Schelling und die Offenbarung* (*Schelling and Revelation*), MEGA, pp. 247–249.

62. Karl Marx and Frederick Engels, *Selected Works* (London: Lawrence and Wishart, 1958), p. 52.

63. Ossip Flechtheim, *The Communist Party of Germany in the Weimar Republic* (Offenbach, 1948)

64. Künzli, *op. cit.*, p. 187.
65. Bertram Wolfe, *Marxism—One Hundred Years in the Life of a Doctrine* (New York: The Dial Press, 1965), p. 32.
66. Karl Marx and Friedrich Engels, *The Russian Menace to Europe* (Glencoe: The Free Press, 1952), p. 63.
67. Quoted by Bertrand Wolfe, *Marxism* (New York: The Dial Press, 1965)
68. Engels, MEW, VI, 176.
68a. *Deutschland Magazine*, February 1985.
69. Quoted by Nathaniel Weyl, *Karl Marx: Racist* (New Rochelle, N.Y.: Arlington House)
70. Karl Marx, MEW, XXXV, 122.
71. Chushichi Tsuzuki, *The Life of Eleanor Marx* (Oxford: Clarendon Press, 1967), p. 85.
72. Frederick Tatford, *The Prince of Darkness* (Eastbourne: Bible & Advent Testimony Movement, 1967)
73. Sergius Martin Riis, *Karl Marx, Master of Fraud* (New York: Robert Speller, 1962), p. 11.
74. Edgar Marx, Letter of 31 March 1854 to Karl Marx, MEW, II, 18.
75. Jenny Marx, Letter (dated after 11 August 1844) to Karl Marx, MEW, Suppl. Vol. I, 652.
76. Franz Mehring, *op. cit.*, p. 18.
77. Franz Mehring, *Karl Marx—The Story of His Life* (New York: Covici, Friede, 1935), p. 32.
78. Karl Marx, Letter of 20 May 1882 to Friedrich Engels, MEW. XXXV. 65.
79. Walter Kaufmann, *Hegel* (Garden City: Doubleday, 1965), p. 288.
80. V. Illitch Lenin, *Complete Works* (Moscow: Political Literature Publishing House, 1964. In Russian), Vol. 48, pp. 226–227.
81. *Ibid.*, Vol. 45, p. 86.
82. *Ibid.*, Vol. 54, pp. 86–87.
83. 'Budilnik', Russia, No. 48, of 1883. Quoted in *The New Review*, New York, 140/1980, p. 276.
84. George Katkov, *The Trial of Bukharin* (London: B. T. Batsford, Ltd., 1969), 1. p. 29.
85. Roy Medvedev, *Let History Judge* (New York: Alfred Knopf, 1971), p. 183.
85a. F. J. Raddatz, *Karl Marx* (Berlin, 1925), p. 32.

85b. Boris Souvarine, *Stalin*.

85c. MEW, XXVII, 292.

86. Milovan Djilas, *Strange Times*, 'Kontinent' 33, p. 25.

87. *Ibid*.

88. Svetlana Alliluyeva, *Twenty Letters to a Friend* (London: Hutchinson, 1967), pp. 64ff.

89. Paloczy Horvath, *Stalin* (Germany: Bertelmannsverlag)

90. Abdurakhman Avtorkhanov, *Criminals in Bolshevism* (Frankfurt-am-Main: Possev Verlag. In Russian), Grani No. 89–90, pp. 324–325.

91. Abdurakhman Avtorkhanov, *The Provenience of Partocracy* (Frankfurt-am-Main: Possev Verlag, 1973. In Russian), pp. 198–201.

92. *Express*, Paris, 6 October 1979.

93. *Tempo*, Italy, 1 November 1979.

94. P. Underwood, *The Vampire's Bedside Companion* (Frewin).

95. H. Knaust, *The Testament of Evil*.

96. Manfred Zach, *Mao Tse-tung* (Esslingen: Bechtle Verlag, 1969), p. 13.

96a. MEW, V, 457.

96b. MEW, XXXI, 191; XXV, 179.

96c. MEW, VI, 283; VI, 286; VI, 279.

96d. Lenin, *Collected Works*, vol. 32, p. 281.

97. Aleksandr I. Solzhenitsyn, *The Gulag Archipelago* (New York: Harper & Row, 1973). Vol. I-II, 173.

98. *Russkaia Misl* (*Russian Thought*), Paris, 13 March 1975. In Russian.

99. Rev. Dr. I. Nahyewsky, 'Spomyny Polovoho Dykhovnyka', *America*, 7 October 1982, Vol. 1XX1, No. 176, pp. 4, 18.

100. V. Ilyich Lenin, *Military Correspondence* (Moscow, 1954), p. 148.

101. Trotsky, *Stalin*, quoted in *Novii Journal*, 158/85.

102. Pierre Daix, *Picasso, the Man and His Work* (Paris: Somogy), p. 8.

103. *Ibid.*, pp. 188–190.

104. Aleister Crowley, *The Book of Thoth* (Berkeley, Koshmarin Press, 1904), p. 97.

105. *Ibid.*, pp. 134, 135.

106. *Ibid.*, p. 137.

107. *Sovietskaia Molodioj (Soviet Youth)*, Moscow, 14 February 1976. In Russian. 'Let They Kingdom Be Destroyed', p. 4.

108. *Rhein-Neckar Zeitung (Rhine-Neckar Newspaper)*, Heidelberg, 5 February 1968. 'Kultusminister antwortet Studentenpfarrer' ('Minister of Cults Answers Youth Pastor')

109. *Paris-Match*, 10 December 1982.

110. *Kommunism Uzvara (Victory of Communism)*, Riga, April 1974. In Lithuanian.

111. Anatolij Levitin-Krasnov, *Böse Jahre (Evil Years)* Lucerne: Rex-Verlag, 1977), pp. 144–145.

112. *Prasvoslavnaia Rus (Orthodox Russia)*, San Francisco, No. 20, 1977. In Russian. 'Satanist Worshippers', pp. 9–12.

113. D. Bacu, *Piteshti* (Madrid: Colectia Dacoromania, 1963), 71, 187. In Romanian.

114. *Cuvantul Romanesc*, Canada, February 1980.

115. Hermann Hartfeld, *Irina* (Chappaqua, N.Y.: Christian Herald Books, 1981)

116. *Theories of Surplus Value*, passage 'The apologist conception of the productivity of all professions', p. 375.

117. A. Reghelson, *The Tragedy of the Russian Church*.

118. *Catacombes*, France, September 1980.

119. Salu Ndebele, *Guerilla for Christ* (New Jersey: Fleming H. Revell), pp. 9–10.

120. *Impact*, Switzerland, February 1981.

121. 'Chronicle of the Lithuanian Catholic Church', No. 44, 1981.

122. Priest Dudko, *O nashem upovanti (About Our Hope)* (Paris: YMCA Press, 1975. In Russian), p. 51.

123. Igor Shafarevitch, *La Legislation sur la religion en URSS (Religious Legislation in the USSR)* (Paris: Seuil, 1974. In French), pp. 67–71.

124. Sheila Ostrander and Lynn Schroder, *Psychic Discoveries Behind the Iron Curtain* (Englewood Cliffs: Prentice Hall, 1970)

125. Novie Russkoie Slovo *(New Russian Language)*, New York, 30 July 1975. In Russian. 'Para-Psychology in the USSR', 2.

126. MEW, II, 9.

127. Bakunin, *Works*, Vol. III, p. 206.
128. Quoted in Arnold Kunzli, *Karl Marx, a Psychography* (Vienna, 1966), p. 403.
129. MEW, XXVII, 107.
130. MEW, XXXII, 351.
131. *Christian News*, 4 March 1985.
132. Montgomery Hyde, *Stalin* (London: Rupert Hart-Davis), pp. 28–29.
133. Karl Markus Michel, *Politische Katechismen: Volney, Kleist, Hess* (*Political Doctrines: Volney, Kleist, Hess*) (Frankfurt-am-Main: Insel Verlag, 1966). *Red Catechism for the German People*, by Moses Hess, pp. 71–73.
134. Hess, Letter of 2 September 1841 to Berthold Auerbach, MEGA, I, i (2) 261.
135. Jung, Letter of 18 October 1841 to Arnold Ruge, *ibid*.
136. Moses Hess, *Rome and Jerusalem* (New York: Philosophical Library, 1958), p. 10.
137. *Ibid.*, p. 15.
138. Moses Hess, *Ausgewählte Schriften* (*Selected Works*), *Rome and Jerusalem* (Cologne: Melzer-Verlag, 1962), p. 229.
139. Hess, *Rome and Jerusalem, ibid.*, p. 18.
140. Hess, *ibid.*, p. 27.
141. Hess, *Ausgewählte Schriften, ibid.*, pp. 236–237.
142. *Ibid.*, p. 308.
143. *Ibid.*, p. 243.
144. *Ibid.*, p. 324.
145. *Kommunistisches Bekenntnis in Fragen und Antworten* (*Communist Credo in Questions and Answers*), *ibid.*, p. 190.
146. *Die eine und ganze Freiheit* (*The One and Only Total Freedom*), *ibid.*, p. 149.
147. *Philosophie der Tat* (*The Philosophy of Action*), *ibid.*, p. 138.
148. Edmund Silberner, *Moses Hess* (Leiden: Brill, 1966), p. 31.
149. *Ibid.*, p. 32.
150. *Ibid.*, p. 121.
151. *Ibid.*, p. 421.
152. Dudko, *op. cit.*, p. 53.
153. Silberner, *op. cit.*, p. 421.

154. *Ibid.*
155. *Ibid.*, p. 418.
156. Moses Hess, *Philosophische Sozialistische Schriften. 13. Ueber das Geldwesen (Philosophical Socialist Writings. About the Monetary System)* (Berlin: Akademie-Verlag, 1961), p. 345.
157. Hess, *Rome and Jerusalem, ibid.*, p. 44.
158. *Ibid.*, p. 10.
159. Moses Hess, *Briefwechsel (Correspondence)*, Letter of 9 December 1863 to Lassalle (The Hague: Mouton & Co., 1959), p. 459.
160. Karl Marx, *Das Kapital (The Capital)*, MEW, XXIII, 779.
161. G. W. F. Hegel, *Werke. Fragment über Volksreligion und Christentum (Works. Fragment on Popular Religious Beliefs and Christianity)* (Frankfurt-am-Main: Suhrkamp Verlag, 1971) I, pp. 35–36.
162. U. Steklov, *M. A. Bakunin, His Life and Activity* (Moscow: Literature Publishing House, 1937), vol. 3, p. 435.
163. Quoted from *The Catechism of the Revolutionist* by Dostoievsky in his *Complete Works*, vol. 12, p. 194.
164. F. M. Dostoievsky, *op. cit.*, *The Demons*, vol. 10, p. 312.
165. *Ibid.*, p. 322.
166. *Ibid.*, p. 324.
167. Volodin, *Tchernishevsky* or Netahaiev (Moscow: Koriakin and Pleeman, 1976), p. 247.
168. V. Burtsev, *During 100 Years: Compendium of the History of Political and Social Movements in Russia* (London, 1897), p. 94.
169. Volodin, *op. cit.*, p. 223.
170. E. S. Vilenskaia, *Revolutionist Underground in Russia* (Moscow, 1965), p. 398.
171. Volodin, *loc. cit.*
172. *Russkaia Misl*, 17 November 1983.
173. Volodin, *op. cit.*, p. 155.
174. P. F. De Villemarest, *Les Pourvoyeurs du Goulag (Gulag Overseers)* (Geneva: Famot, 1976), vol. III, pp. 233ff. In French.
175. Dr. Lawrence Pazder, *Michelle Remembers* (New York: Condon & Littes, 1982).

176. *Selections from Nietzsche* (New York: Viking, 1954), p. 600.
177. *Weekly World News*, 2 February 1983.
178. *Iunii Kommunist*, Moscow, December 1984.
179. David Rjazanov, *Karl Marx als Denker, Mensch und Revolutionär* (*Karl Marx: Man, Thinker and Revolutionist*) (Vienna: Verlag für Literatur und Politik, 1928), pp. 149–150.
180. Künzli, *op. cit.*, p. 352.
181. Moshe Glickson, *The Jewish Complex of Karl Marx* (New York: Herzl Press, Pamphlet No. 20, 1961), p. 40.
182. Künzli, *op. cit.*, p. 361.
183. *Ibid.*, pp. 372–373.
184. Karl Marx, Letter of 16 January 1861 to Lassalle, MEW, XXX, 578.
185. Payne, *op. cit.*, p. 306.
186. William Tyndale, *Works* (Parker So., 1849), quoted by the *Oxford English Dictionary* (Oxford: Clarendon Press, 1933), vol. VIII, p. 735.
187. William Shakespeare, *Complete Works* (Glenview: Scott, Foresman, 1973), *Midsummer Night's Dream*, Act II, Scene I, 33–34, p. 189.
188. *Svenska Dagbladet* (*Swedish Daily News*), Stockholm, 17 January 1948. *An Unforgettable Night*, by Alexei Stjusev. In Swedish.
189. Solzhenitsyn, *op. cit.*, vol. III-IV, p. 10.
190. *Nauka I Religia* (*Science and Religion*), Moscow, December 1976. In Russian. Wurmbrand on the Lecturing Trip. Vol. 12, pp. 73–76.
191. *Idea*, 3 June 1983.
192. *Osservatore Romano*, 17 September 1978.
193. Quoted in Gerhard Zacharias, *The Cult of Satan and the Black Mass*.
194. INF of *Aide à l'Église en détresse*, April-June 1980.

# Other Marshall Pickering Paperbacks

## THE TORN VEIL

*Sister Gulshan and Thelma Sangster*

Gulshan Fatima was brought up in a Muslim Sayed family according to the orthodox Islamic code of the Shias.
Suffering from a crippling paralysis she travelled to England in search of medical help. Although unsuccessful in medical terms, this trip marked the beginning of a spiritual awakening that led ultimately to her conversion to Christianity.
Gulshan and her father also travelled to Mecca in the hope that God would heal her, but that trip too was of no avail. However, Gulshan was not detered. She relentlessly pursued God and He faithfully answered her prayers. Her conversion, when it came, was dramatic and brought with a miraculous healing.
**The Torn Veil** is Sister Gulshan's thrilling testimony to the power of God which can break through every barrier.

## RELEASE
## The Miracle of the Siberian Seven

*Timothy Chmykhalov with Danny Smith*

The plight of the 'Siberian Seven' attracted widespread publicity and support.
Timothy Chmykhalov, youngest member of the seven, vividly recounts the events leading to the entry into the US Embassy in 1978, the long years of hoping and waiting, the uncertainty which faced them when they left in 1983 and finally the freedom which they found in America.
**Release** is a powerful testimony of faith and courage amidst intense pressure and threat of persecution. A story of hope and determination in the face of much discouragement.

If you wish to receive *regular information* about *new books,* please send your name and address to:

London Bible Warehouse
PO Box 123
Basingstoke
Hants RG23 7NL

Name _____

Address _____

_____

_____

_____

I am especially interested in:
- [ ] Biographies
- [ ] Fiction
- [ ] Christian living
- [ ] Issue related books
- [ ] Academic books
- [ ] Bible study aids
- [ ] Children's books
- [ ] Music
- [ ] Other subjects

P.S. If you have ideas for new Christian Books or other products, please write to us too!